katy holder

good food outdoors

recipes for picnics, barbecues,
camping and road trips

Hardie Grant

EXPLORE

Contents

Introduction

Most of us are social creatures who love spending downtime with family and friends for a healthy dose of fun, laughter and, of course, delicious food.

Getting together isn't just about meeting in restaurants and cafes or gathering for dinner parties at home – there is so much fun to be had eating outside as well. With the pandemic forcing us to spend more time at home – restricting travel, eating out, inviting people to our homes and gathering in large groups – many of us are craving social interaction like never before. Whatever the future holds, whether we go back to our old ways or find a new normal, eating outdoors will always be a great way to get together.

This book is a collection of recipes for anyone who loves being and eating outdoors, although everything can also be eaten (and cooked) inside. Maybe you love picnics, hosting a barbecue, going on a hike or a road trip, or simply getting away from it all to camp under the stars. Or perhaps afternoon tea or brunch is more your style. Using the recipes in this book, there'll be nothing stopping you. Good Food Outdoors is full of inspiring recipes that look good, taste great and, if required, travel well too.

Let's take this opportunity to explore the great outdoors, not only on longer road trips and camping trips, but also closer to home. It's time to make new discoveries and see our neighbourhood, local parks and even our own backyard in a new light. So throw down a picnic rug, fire up the barbecue, put up a tent or do whatever suits you and let's enjoy good food outdoors.

Katy

Tips and tricks for eating outdoors

To ensure your food arrives at your destination in the best condition possible, it's a good idea to give a little thought to how you transport and store it.

Picnics and day trips

Having a picnic or going for a hike with friends and family is a great way to get everyone together – outside. A picnic can range from a simple collection of sandwiches and a sweet treat or two to a lavish affair of a smorgasbord filled with baguettes, dips, small bites, quiches, pies and delicious desserts. A picnic also generally means that everyone contributes to the meal, rather than one person having to do everything. If you are going for a hike and have to carry your food, some simple and delicious sandwiches and snacks may be the way to go. Whichever you choose, this book provides plenty of great recipes.

Keeping your food cold

Always remember to keep things cold in a cool box when you are transporting your food. It's worth investing in a good-quality cool box to ensure your food can stay chilled for several hours. Never leave food in the back of a hot car, and when you arrive at your destination, always place your cool box in the coolest or shadiest spot out of direct sunlight until serving. If you are going on a hike, consider packing your food in a cool bag, or choose food that can survive the day in a backpack.

Transporting your food

Transporting food for a picnic or bring-a-plate occasion is often the trickiest part. There's nothing worse than lovingly preparing a dish to find it's fallen apart or been damaged while you were on the move. For many of the recipes, you will find suggestions on how best to transport dishes to avoid such scenarios.

In general, if transporting pies, tartlets and cakes, cool them on a wire rack then return them to the tin for moving; this will help prevent damage while on the move, particularly to fragile pastry. Wrap sandwiches in layers of baking paper and tie the ends with string or coloured twine.

It's often a better idea to cut cakes, pies and tortillas on arrival. However if this isn't possible, transport individual pieces between layers of baking paper, padded with paper towel if necessary.

For salads, don't dress them too far in advance, otherwise the leaves will become soggy. Transporting the salad components separately before tossing everything together at the last minute will ensure your salad looks its best when served. Why not divide a salad among individual cardboard noodle boxes (available from most craft shops) before you leave home, and then dress the salads just before serving? The boxes prevent the ingredients getting squashed, although make sure you don't cram too much into each box.

Ensure containers carrying liquids, such as sauces or salad dressings, are airtight and leakproof; you can wrap them in a layer of plastic wrap to be extra safe.

Serving your food

Think about how you're going to serve your food and see if this can make transportation easier. With the ever-increasing focus on sustainability, instead of taking disposable plastic or paper cutlery and crockery, consider investing in a beautiful melamine set. If you really need to use disposable products, ensure you buy bamboo or other recycled, recyclable or compostable products. And look around your kitchen and house for other interesting containers you can use to transport and serve your food in.

Barbecues

Barbecues often mean casual dining, but they can be anything – from a simple affair to enjoy on a glorious summer's day to a once-a-year occasion for a big celebration. Due to their often casual nature, they can be organised at the last minute, depending on weather and which of your friends are around. The food can range from a marinated butterflied leg of lamb to kebabs, burgers or fish fillets. Add a few sides and salads and some bread rolls, and you've got yourself a party. You can, of course keep your table setting casual and simple, but if you're up for it and have the time, why not have a bit of fun styling your table (*see* page XI for some simple styling ideas).

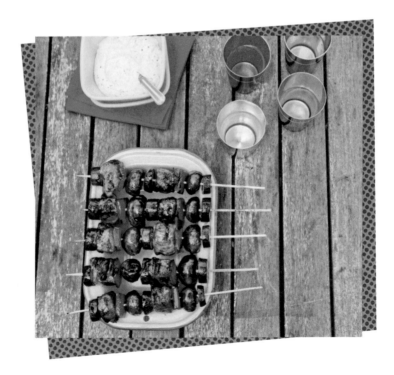

Styling your picnic or barbecue

Although the simple act of sharing food is in itself a lovely thing to do, styling your picnic or barbecue takes it up a notch. There are so many simple but effective ideas that you can use to personalise your table setting or picnic.

Be inspired by nature. This can be as simple as placing some beautiful weathered branches in the centre of your table, or using a smooth river pebble to prevent your paper napkins flying away in the wind.

Beautiful styling doesn't mean you need to go out and buy new things; look for inspiration in what you already have. A few pieces of vintage cutlery will add instant glamour or quirkiness to the table. I have a collection of teaspoons that I bring out for afternoon tea; I love the fact that none of them match and have fond memories of where each one was bought.

Old glass bottles and mason jars can be used in a multitude of ways. Use them to transport food or to hold a flower arrangement, fill them with pretty or colourful sweets, or serve drinks in them. They don't even need to be old – some drinks come in gorgeous bottles that make cute vases. Lots of small bottles holding just one or two flower stems each can create a bigger impact than one large floral arrangement.

Baking paper and old-fashioned twine or coloured string add an old-world charm to picnics and table settings. Instead of simply wrapping sandwiches or rolls in foil, wrap them in baking paper and tie with beautiful string – when you hand them out it's like you're handing over a homemade gift to unwrap.

I'm a huge fan of typography and have a set of alphabet stamps that I use in myriad ways, such as to stamp a name on a luggage tag to tie around a napkin or to write fun words on a smooth stone to hold down napkins or place on the table.

Camping and road trips

Due to global travel restrictions during the pandemic, the number of people loading up their cars and heading off on a camping trip or road trip has increased dramatically. But camping doesn't need to mean canned and freeze-dried foods or cheap sausages in a roll. On our camping trips we eat like kings.

There are a variety of ways to cook your food when you are camping – over an open fire, using a gas cooker or on a barbecue.

If you plan to camp a lot, then a camp oven, or Dutch oven, is a very worthwhile investment. A camp oven is a cast-iron casserole dish that can be used for all your one-pot meals that are cooked over a fire, and with a little know-how you can use it to cook, fry, roast and bake, meaning it can be used for everything from soups, stews and roasts to breads and cakes.

As I see it, a camp oven works almost like your entire home stove and you can't achieve the same effect with a gas cooker. Although I do have two camp ovens – a smaller and a larger one – one camp oven should be sufficient for your camping needs. If you are only going to use it for your family then don't go too large. However, if you plan to always be cooking for groups, then get a slightly bigger one. Canvas carriers can be bought from camping stores and will help keep your oven in good condition. Also see the camp oven guide on page XVIII for tips on getting the most out of your camp oven. I generally don't advise using a camp oven over gas, largely because I tend to use my camp oven for slow cooking and it would use too much gas. However, this doesn't mean they can't be. If you only have a camp oven, you can place it over your gas cooker and use it for boiling, frying and quick stews.

Keeping food cold

When camping, you need to give careful consideration to how you will transport and store your chilled food. Not everyone is lucky enough to own a car fridge, so putting a little thought into how you pack your chilled food before you go will not only help keep your food cold, but also make finding and keeping things in good condition easier. If you live in a hot climate or want to stay away for several days at a time, it's worth investing in a good-quality cool box. Use good quality ice packs and leave room at the top of your cool box for a layer of them, as the cool air will sink down. If you are using bags of ice, be aware there are usually holes in the bags. Ensure your food is either in waterproof containers or tightly shut resealable bags, or you will end up with a mess of waterlogged food. Many larger cool boxes have bungs on the side to empty the water, and it's best to do this every day.

If going for more than a couple of days, you can freeze milk, juice and packets of bacon, sausages and meat before you leave. Not only does this make them last longer without going off, but the frozen packets also act as additional ice packs. Defrost in the cool box, never in the sun. If you have some fresh meat that isn't going to last another day, cook it, then chill it and eat it the next day for lunch.

Many butchers will vacuum pack meat for a small charge, so ask about this when buying meat. Although the meat will still need to be stored in a cool box, it should last for an extra three to four days longer than unsealed meats. Vacuum sealers have also become very affordable these days, so if you go camping often, consider investing in one. Having your own means you can marinate and pack meat from home, ready to cook, and it can be used to pack and freeze entire home-cooked meals, so all you need to do is reheat them at the campsite.

Pack cheeses into sturdy containers to prevent them getting squashed. Do the same with packets of meats that aren't frozen. Keep things well wrapped to prevent cross-contamination, and to avoid waterlogged food if you're packing your cool box with ice.

Eggs can be tricky to transport, and I don't find the plastic camping egg cartons especially effective. If I'm only taking a few, I pack them in a plastic container padded with paper towel, which I can then use as a napkin – waste not want not! If I'm taking more, I transport the eggs in the cartons and always ensure they are on the top.

I transport many vegetables, such as avocados, cucumbers, tomatoes and salad leaves, in plastic containers, although it all depends on how many days I'm going for and how full my cool box gets. Tomatoes and avocados don't need to be refrigerated, so that can save you space if necessary.

Packing non-perishable foods

Packing the food not stored inside your cool box should also be well planned. Think about decanting ingredients such as sugar, coffee and flour into smaller containers before you leave, based on how long you will be away and how many people you will need to feed. Then, using a washable marker, write the contents on the top of the container, as more often than not you'll be rummaging in boxes to find things and the lid will be the easiest to spot. Stick white labels on tops of spice jars to easily spot them in your food stocks.

Using a camp oven over coals

Camp ovens are incredibly versatile. By dividing the coals between the top and bottom and also around the base of the camp oven in different ways and amounts, you can supply heat to mimic almost all cooking styles, including boiling, baking, frying and roasting. This is a general guide on how to divide the coals for different cooking methods. I've found that my camp oven can get very hot on the bottom, so I tend to only place a couple of coals underneath my camp oven and place the rest around it to avoid burning the food on the bottom.

You certainly don't want to get stressed when cooking over a fire. The whole idea of campfire cooking is that you are relaxed, it should be fun and there are few time constraints (except maybe that the kids need to be fed!). Start your fire mid to late afternoon so you have plenty of coals to use when it comes to cooking. You want to be cooking over coals, not flames.

Imagine the coals are like the knob on your stovetop. Less coals/cooler coals equals lower heat. Need a bit more heat? Replenish the coals or add more. I prefer to use coals from my campfire, but you can also use briquettes to get more control over the heat (you can find guides and charts online if you want to try and achieve more accurate temperatures). The benefit of a camp oven is that you can easily make adjustments by moving coals around. My best advice is to check the coals and your food often, to make sure the food is still cooking but not burning.

Use a spade to move the coals around. I use about one spadeful on the top of the camp oven, and then I shovel coals around the base to create an oven effect. For baking and for low heat (depending on the size of your camp oven), I put about ⅓ of a spadeful underneath the camp oven as well.

BOILING AND FRYING	BAKING	ROASTING	BROILING
Heat division All coals underneath. When low–medium heat required, use fewer underneath and place coals around the base of the camp oven.	**Heat division** Most coals on top, with some around the base and just a few underneath.	**Heat division** Put coals on top, then pile coals around the outside, up to about a quarter of the way up.	**Heat division** All on top.
Use this technique for stovetop cooking, such as boiling, sautéing, searing, stewing, simmering, stir-frying and deep-frying.	By adding most of the coals on top of the lid, you can use your camp oven to bake bread, cakes and baked dishes.	Divide plenty of heat evenly to roast meat and vegetables.	This technique is good for making crispy toppings.

Top tips

- Season your camp oven well before use.
- Use a spade to distribute the coals evenly.
- Check the coals often to ensure they're still going.
- Don't use too many coals underneath. For baking and simmering you really don't need much, so move some of the coals around the camp oven instead to avoid your food burning to the bottom.
- Check the food often and move coals around if necessary.
- Use proper equipment to handle the hot camp oven. Use a pot lifter tool (available from camping stores) to remove the lid or to move the oven around in the coals. It's also a good idea to wear heatproof gloves.
- Be careful when taking off the lid with coals on it, and keep a rock or branch close by to rest it on. Never put your lid down on the ground or the base will get dirty.
- Never leave the hot lid lying around for someone to step on.
- Don't wash your camp oven with soap - ever. Always clean your oven soon after using it. Empty any remaining food, add some water then bring to the boil on the fire. I use a gentle scrubber to remove any tough bits. Empty the water, put the oven by the fire to dry, then add a light coating of oil to re-season.

How to use this book

Vegetarian and vegan recipes

When getting together for a meal, it's important to remember to cater for any vegans or vegetarians. Vegetarian and vegan dishes have been marked with a **V** symbol on top of the recipe so you can easily find them. There are also many recipes that can easily be made vegetarian or vegan – look for the **MAKE IT VEG** tag for suggestions for what to leave out and what to add.

Gluten-free recipes

When it comes to gluten, the number one rule is: always check the label. Gluten is a protein that is found in products that contain wheat, rye and barley. Oats are actually gluten-free, but because of the way they're processed, there is a chance of cross-contamination. Besides the more obvious things like bread and pasta, there's a whole range of products on the supermarket shelves that often contain gluten, including soy sauce, hoisin sauce, sweet chilli sauce, baking powder and worcestershire sauce. Generally, it's possible to find gluten-free versions of these ingredients, so pretty much every one of these recipes can be made gluten-free.

Some of the recipes that are already gluten-free in this book include: Prosciutto-wrapped shrimp with aïoli (*see* page 14); Manchego and olive tortilla (*see* page 17); Marinated butterflied leg of lamb (*see* page 42); Marinated pork loin with Greek salad (*see* page 46); Easy fish and vegetable stew (*see* page 54); One-pot roast chicken with vegetables (*see* page 58); Vegetable and chickpea casserole (*see* page 62); Chargrilled zucchini, onion and feta salad (*see* page 72); Quinoa salad with goat's cheese, basil and crisp prosciutto (*see* page 74); Pistachio meringues with caramel filling (*see* page 102); and Strawberry and passionfruit meringue cake (*see* page 109).

Make it at home

Some of the recipes in this book, especially those in the One-pot camping dishes chapter, are more often cooked in a camp oven over coals from a campfire (*see* page XVI for a guide). But don't worry, I've provided instructions for how to cook them at home as well.

Conversion charts

Measuring cups and tablespoons vary slightly around the world, but generally the difference isn't enough to affect a recipe unless you're baking. This book uses Australian cups and tablespoons. An Australian and New Zealand metric cup holds 250 ml/8 fl oz and a tablespoon holds 20 ml/¾ fl oz.

In the US a cup holds about 237 ml/8 fl oz, and in North America, UK and New Zealand tablespoons hold 15 ml/½ fl oz.

Liquid measurements

METRIC CUP	METRIC	IMPERIAL	METRIC	IMPERIAL
¼ cup	60 ml	2 fl oz	30 g	1 oz
⅓ cup	80 ml	2½ fl oz	100 g	3½ oz
½	125 ml	4 fl oz	450 g	1 lb
⅔	170 ml	5½ fl oz	500 g	1 lb 2 oz
¾	185 ml	6 fl oz	600 g	1 lb 5 oz
1	250 ml	8½ fl oz	1 kg	2 lb 3 oz

Oven temperatures

I've used fan-forced oven temperatures throughout this book. If you use a conventional oven, simply add about 20°C (70°F) or use the table below as a guide. Remember, no two ovens are the same, so it's best to check your food often.

FAN-FORCED	CONVENTIONAL	GAS MARK
120°C (250°F)	140°C (275°F)	1
130°C (265°F)	150°C (300°F)	2
140°C (275°F)	160°C (320°F)	
150°C (300°F)	170°C (340°F)	3
160°C (320°F)	180°C (350°F)	4
170°C (340°F)	190°C (375°F)	5
180°C (350°F)	200°C (400°F)	6
200°C (400°F)	220°C (430°F)	7

Mini morsels

&

bigger bites

Shrimp cakes with cucumber dipping sauce

These shrimp cakes are delicious eaten hot or cold. If going on a picnic, chill them before leaving and keep them chilled until it's time to eat. For a barbecue, take them raw and cook them on-site, serving them hot. You could also try wrapping them in lettuce leaves to serve.

500 g (1 lb 2 oz) raw shrimp (prawns), peeled and deveined

2 teaspoons finely chopped lemongrass, white part only

3 makrut (kaffir) lime leaves, finely chopped

1 small red or green chilli, deseeded and finely chopped

2 teaspoons lime juice

2 teaspoons fish sauce

1 free-range egg white

2 tablespoons chopped coriander (cilantro) leaves

2 tablespoons chopped mint

40 g (1½ oz/⅔ cup) panko (Japanese breadcrumbs) (see Tip)

vegetable oil, for brushing

Cucumber dipping sauce

2 tablespoons caster (superfine) sugar

1 Lebanese (short) cucumber

1 small red Asian shallot or French shallot, thinly sliced

1 small red chilli, sliced into thin rings

1 tablespoon rice vinegar

1. Put the shrimp into the bowl of a food processor and pulse for about 10 seconds until roughly chopped. Add the lemongrass, lime leaves, chilli, lime juice, fish sauce, egg white, coriander and mint. Pulse for about 10 seconds more, or until just combined. Do not over-process.

2. Transfer to a bowl and stir in the panko. Slightly wet your hands to make handling the mixture easier, then form into 16 small patty shapes, about 5 cm (2 in) in diameter. Place the patties in a single layer on a plate, then chill in the fridge for 30 minutes.

3. Meanwhile, make the dipping sauce. Put the sugar in a small bowl with a large pinch of salt and add 2 tablespoons hot water, stirring to dissolve the sugar. Leave to cool.

4. Peel the cucumber, halve it lengthways, scrape out the seeds using a teaspoon, then dice. Place the cucumber, shallot and chilli in a small serving dish, or divide them among a couple of smaller dishes. Stir the vinegar into the cooled sugar liquid, then pour this liquid over the vegetables.

5. Heat a chargrill pan over medium heat. Brush the shrimp patties lightly with vegetable oil and cook for 2–3 minutes on each side, until lightly browned and cooked through. Drain on paper towel. The patties can be eaten hot, warm or cold, accompanied by the dipping sauce.

6. If transporting, arrange the shrimp cakes in single layers between sheets of baking paper. Take the dressing in an airtight container.

Mini meatballs with herb dipping sauce

Makes about 40

Meatballs are a favourite with young and old alike. I like to make lots of little one-bite balls, but you can make them bigger if you prefer. The dipping sauce is a delicious accompaniment, although you might find your younger guests munching on just the meatballs!

2 tablespoons olive oil, plus extra for frying

1 small red onion, finely chopped

3 garlic cloves, crushed

1–2 tablespoons harissa paste

1 kg (2 lb 3 oz) minced (ground) lamb

2 tablespoons finely chopped flat-leaf (Italian) parsley

2 tablespoons finely chopped mint

finely grated zest of 1 lemon

30 g (1 oz/½ cup) panko (Japanese breadcrumbs) (*see* Tip page 3)

Herb dipping sauce

80 ml (2½ fl oz/⅓ cup) olive oil

2 tablespoons lemon juice

large handful coriander (cilantro) leaves, finely chopped

large handful flat-leaf (Italian) parsley, finely chopped

2 garlic cloves, crushed

1. Heat 1 tablespoon of the oil in a frying pan and gently fry the onion and garlic for about 5 minutes, without browning. Transfer to a large bowl and add the harissa paste, lamb, herbs, lemon zest and panko. Season well with sea salt and freshly ground black pepper. Mix with your hands for about 2 minutes, or until the mixture turns a slightly paler pink.

2. Form the meatball mixture into about 40 small balls, each the size of a walnut (or larger if you prefer). Chill in the fridge for 30 minutes.

3. Meanwhile, make the dipping sauce. Whisk the oil and lemon juice together, then stir in the remaining ingredients.

4. Heat the remaining 1 tablespoon of oil in a large frying pan. Add a batch of meatballs, taking care not to overcrowd the pan. Allow the meatballs to form a crust before turning; cook for about 10 minutes, or until browned all over and cooked through. Cook the remaining meatballs, in batches if necessary, adding a little extra oil as needed.

5. If preferred, the meatballs can be cooked at your destination. Serve the meatballs hot, warm or cold with the dipping sauce on the side. Offer toothpicks to serve, if desired.

Sesame-crusted tuna with wasabi mayonnaise dip

Make sure you don't overcook the tuna in this recipe, as the cubes of fish will continue to cook as they cool. When crumbing or coating, it's always a good idea to start with half the crumb, then replenish when needed; this prevents the crumb ingredients becoming soggy in the crumbing process. Wasabi is deceptively fiery, so don't be tempted to add too much, and ensure it is well stirred into the mayonnaise.

3 fresh tuna steaks (about 700 g/1 lb 9 oz)

125 ml (4 fl oz/½ cup) olive oil, approximately

100 g (3½ oz) sesame seeds (mix of black and white)

½–1 teaspoon freshly ground black pepper

Wasabi mayonnaise

½–1 teaspoon wasabi

185 g (6½ oz/¾ cup) Japanese mayonnaise or good-quality egg mayonnaise

1 teaspoon mirin (available from the Asian section in most supermarkets or Asian stores)

1 teaspoon soy sauce

1 teaspoon rice vinegar or white wine vinegar

1. Cut each tuna steak into 2 cm (¾ in) cubes. Pour about 2 tablespoons of the oil into a shallow dish. Add half the tuna cubes and toss gently to coat.

2. Put half the sesame seeds in a separate shallow dish and add half the black pepper. Roll the oiled tuna cubes in the seed mixture, until they are completely coated. Gently coat the remaining tuna in the same dish of oil, then coat in the remaining seeds and pepper.

3. Heat about 5 mm (¼ in) of oil in a medium, heavy-based frying pan over medium–high heat. Add the tuna in batches, taking care not to overcrowd the pan. Fry for about 1½ minutes, turning regularly; the cubes should still be pink in the middle, as they'll continue to cook once out of the pan. Drain on paper towel and leave to cool.

4. To make the wasabi mayonnaise, put the wasabi in a bowl and gradually whisk in the mayonnaise, followed by the remaining ingredients.

5. If transporting, layer the tuna between sheets of baking paper, and transport the wasabi mayo in an airtight container. Serve with toothpicks on the side for picking up the tuna (*see* Tip).

TIP
Party-ware
stores and Asian
stores often
stock interesting
toothpicks or
mini skewers; pick
up a packet when
you see them.

Smoked salmon and roasted red capsicum pâté on toast

Serves 6

This creamy smoked salmon pâté served on crisp toast triangles is perfect finger food. You can make the pâté smooth or slightly chunky, depending on whether you blend the capsicum into the mix. If you stir the capsicum through after blending, the resulting pâté will be a little creamier.

1 small red capsicum (bell pepper), halved, seeds and membrane removed (or 50 g/1¾ oz bought chargrilled capsicum, drained)

200 g (7 oz) smoked salmon

200 g (7 oz) cream cheese

100 g (3½ oz) sour cream

4 tablespoons finely chopped dill

60–80 ml (2–2½ fl oz/ ¼–⅓ cup) lemon juice

8 thin slices of wholegrain or wholemeal (whole-wheat) bread

1. Preheat a grill (broiler) to high. Squash the capsicum halves to flatten them, then place under the hot grill, skin side up. Grill until the skin is completely blackened. Place in a plastic bag, seal the bag and leave for 15 minutes. Rub or peel off the skin (do not rinse), then finely dice the capsicum and set aside.

2. Put the smoked salmon, cream cheese, sour cream, dill and 60 ml (2 fl oz/¼ cup) of the lemon juice into the bowl of a food processor. Blend for about 20 seconds. Season with sea salt and freshly ground black pepper to taste and add the extra tablespoon of lemon juice if needed. Now either add the diced capsicum and blend for 10 seconds, or transfer the pâté to a bowl and stir in the diced capsicum. Chill the mixture in the fridge for about 30 minutes to firm up slightly.

3. Heat the oven to 180°C (350°F) fan-forced and place a baking sheet in the oven to heat up. Remove the crusts from the bread, then roll the slices out thinly using a rolling pin or bottle. Cut each piece into four triangles. Place on the baking sheet and bake for 8–10 minutes, until golden and crisp. Set aside to cool.

4. Transport the toasts in an airtight container. The pâté can be transported in the either the bowl it was chilled in or in an airtight container. Or if you have some small glass jars, divide it up into individual portions. It will last 3–4 days in the fridge.

TIP
Kecap manis is a thick, dark, sweetened soy sauce available from Asian stores. If you can't find it, simply stir 1 tablespoon of brown sugar into 2 tablespoons of soy sauce instead.

Sichuan beef rice paper rolls

Makes 8

Sichuan (also known as szechuan or szechwan) pepper has a slightly citrusy flavour and produces a tingling, mouth numbing effect; you'll find it in Asian stores and some supermarkets. Rice paper rolls are fun to make, so if you're taking these to someone's house, you could take all the components separately and get everyone to roll their own.

250 g (9 oz) beef eye fillet

1-2 tablespoons olive oil

2 teaspoons sichuan peppercorns

2 tablespoons kecap manis (see Tip)

1 tablespoon lime juice

2 teaspoons sesame oil

8 rice paper wrappers

8 small crunchy lettuce leaves

2 carrots, cut into thin batons

2 Lebanese (short) cucumbers, cut into batons

handful coriander (cilantro) leaves

8 garlic chives, cut in half

Tangy dipping sauce

1 tablespoon fish sauce

1 tablespoon lime juice

1 teaspoon rice vinegar

1 teaspoon sesame oil

2 teaspoons sugar

1 small red chilli, deseeded and finely chopped

MAKE IT VEG

Replace the beef with strips of flavoured firm tofu or slices of avocado.

1. Heat a chargrill pan or barbecue to high. Brush the beef all over with the oil, then cook for 2-3 minutes on each side, or until done to your liking. If the fillets are thick, cook it for a minute on the edges as well. Set aside to cool. Once cool, slice very thinly against the grain.

2. Meanwhile, toast the sichuan peppercorns in a frying pan for 1-2 minutes over medium–high heat, until aromatic, shaking the pan regularly, then crush them using a spice grinder or mortar and pestle until quite fine. Tip into a bowl.

3. Add the kecap manis, lime juice and sesame oil to the crushed sichuan peppercorns. Add the beef slices and toss to coat, then set aside.

4. Whisk together the dipping sauce ingredients, ensuring the sugar dissolves.

5. Briefly dip one rice paper wrapper in a large shallow bowl of warm water. Do not leave it in for too long, or it may tear. Allow the excess water to drip off.

6. Place the wrapper on a board and put a lettuce leaf horizontally in the middle, one-third up from the bottom. Top with 3-4 pieces of carrot, three cucumber batons and a few slices of beef, then several coriander leaves. Fold the end closest to you over the filling, then fold in the sides. Put two garlic chive halves along the seam, with about 4 cm (1½ in) sticking out, then roll up quite tightly. Repeat with the remaining wrappers, keeping the assembled ones under damp paper towel to stop them drying out. Store under damp paper towel in the fridge or a cool box.

7. Divide the sauce among a couple of serving bowls and serve when ready.

Smoky Mexican chicken

Chipotle chillies add a delicious spicy, smoky flavour to food. They're often sold in tins or jars in adobo sauce and are available in many supermarkets and from delis, specialist food stores and online shops. The chillies will be either whole or chopped – both are suitable.

2 tablespoons olive oil, plus extra for greasing

1 tablespoon brown sugar

2 tablespoons apple juice

1 chipotle chilli in adobo sauce, finely chopped, and 2 teaspoons of adobo sauce (or 1 tablespoon if using chopped chipotle chilli in adobo sauce)

2 garlic cloves, crushed

1 teaspoon dried oregano

500–600 g (1 lb 2 oz–1 lb 5 oz) boneless, skinless chicken thighs, preferably free-range, cut in half

lime wedges, to serve

1. Combine the oil, sugar, apple juice, chilli, adobo sauce, garlic and oregano in a bowl and season with sea salt and freshly ground black pepper. Add the chicken and toss to coat. Cover and leave to marinate in the fridge for at least 1 hour, or up to 4 hours.

2. Remove the chicken from the marinade, allowing any excess marinade to drip off.

3. Brush a barbecue or chargrill pan with oil, then heat to medium–high. Cook the chicken for 5–6 minutes on each side, or until cooked through. Cut into smaller pieces to serve, if you like. Serve hot or cold, with lime wedges on the side.

4. If you're taking these to a place that has a barbecue, take them raw and cook on arrival.

TIP
When eating outside, the wind can sometimes carry your napkins away! Solve this problem by tying some colourful string or twine around an interesting-shaped rock, and use this to hold the napkins in place.

Prosciutto-wrapped shrimp with aïoli

Once cooked, these shrimp are dipped into a homemade aïoli. You could, of course, buy a jar of aïoli, but your homemade version will taste far superior. If you're taking these to a place where there's a barbecue, prepare them before you leave, then cook them on arrival. Otherwise, cook them beforehand and eat cold.

20 large raw shrimp (prawns), peeled and deveined, tails left on

100 g (3½ oz) prosciutto

olive oil, for brushing

Aïoli

3 garlic cloves, roughly chopped

1 teaspoon sea salt

2 free-range egg yolks, at room temperature

250 ml (8½ fl oz/1 cup) mild-flavoured olive oil

3–4 teaspoons lemon juice

1. Soak 20 wooden skewers, preferably about 20 cm (8 in) long, in water for 20 minutes.

2. To make the aïoli, put the garlic in a medium bowl with the salt. Using the back of a fork, mash the garlic and salt together until it forms a paste.

3. Add the egg yolks and, using an electric hand mixer, mix until a thick paste forms. With the mixer in motion, start adding the oil, drop by drop; don't be tempted to add it faster, otherwise the aïoli may split. Once the aïoli becomes thick and creamy, you can add the oil in a steady stream. (This process should take 10–15 minutes, so don't rush it.) Add lemon juice to taste and check the seasoning, adding extra salt if needed. Keep in the fridge until required.

4. Thread each shrimp lengthways onto a wooden skewer. Cut the prosciutto into long strips about 3 cm (1¼ in) wide, then, starting just above the tail, wrap a strip around each shrimp, leaving 1 cm (½ in) of shrimp visible at the top. Brush with oil.

5. Cook the shrimp on a chargrill pan or on the flat plate of a barbecue for about 2 minutes on each side, or until the shrimp are cooked through. Serve the shrimp hot, warm or cold with the aïoli dipping sauce.

6. If transporting, the prosciutto-wrapped shrimp can be taken uncooked and then cooked at your destination, or cook and chill them before you go. Transport in a lidded container in a cool box.

Manchego and olive tortilla

Serves 6–8

This substantial tortilla is made with sliced potatoes, creamy crème fraîche and rich manchego cheese. It's easy to transport and then slice on arrival.

850 g (1 lb 14 oz) potatoes, peeled and thinly sliced

10 free-range eggs, lightly beaten

150 g (5½ oz) crème fraîche or sour cream

small handful flat-leaf (Italian) parsley, roughly chopped

150 g (5½ oz) manchego cheese, grated

50 g (1¾ oz) pitted green olives, roughly chopped

green salad, to serve

onion jam (*see* page 26) or chutney, to serve (optional)

1. Preheat the oven to 170°C (340°F) fan-forced. Line the base and side of a 22 cm (8¾ in) springform or loose-based cake tin with a layer of foil, then a layer of baking paper.

2. Cook the potato slices for 5 minutes in boiling, salted water to soften them. Drain well. Leave to cool slightly, then layer half the slices in the base of the tin.

3. Combine the eggs, crème fraîche and parsley and season well with sea salt and freshly ground black pepper. Pour about half the mixture over the potatoes, then scatter with half the cheese and all the olives. Scatter the remaining cheese over the olives, top with the remaining potato slices, then pour the remaining egg mixture over the top.

4. Bake for 40–45 minutes, or until firm, set and golden. Cool for 10 minutes in the tin, then very carefully open the side of the tin, leaving the side around the tortilla to make it easier to reattach before transporting. Leave to cool completely.

5. For easy transportation, carefully close the side of the tin around the base again. Slice into wedges on arrival, and serve with a fresh green salad. Onion jam or chutney makes a delicious accompaniment.

Loaves, breads, pies & muffins

Tuna and egg pan bagnat

Serves 4 (or 6 as a snack)

Pan bagnat is a sandwich from the Nice region of France and is sold in pretty much every market and bakery in the area, usually in a round roll. It's ideal to take on a hike or even a stroll to your local park for a picnic, because the flavours develop as you walk. It often contains anchovies, so feel free to add some of those too if you like.

3 free-range eggs

80 ml (2½ fl oz/⅓ cup) olive oil

2 tablespoons red wine vinegar

1 teaspoon dijon mustard

1 long baguette, about 50–60 cm (16–20 in)

1 garlic clove, cut in half

1 small green capsicum (bell pepper), seeds and membrane removed, thinly sliced

1 tomato, thinly sliced

185 g (6½ oz) tin tuna (in oil or spring water), drained and flaked

20 pitted kalamata olives, cut in half

1. Cook the eggs in boiling water for 7½ minutes. Plunge into cold water to stop them cooking. Cool, peel, then carefully cut into wedges.

2. Whisk together the olive oil, vinegar and mustard until well combined. Season with sea salt and freshly ground black pepper.

3. Slice the baguette in half lengthways and remove a little of the dough from the bottom half to form a hollow. Brush both cut sides of the bread with a little of the olive oil dressing, then rub it with the cut side of the garlic all over as well.

4. Arrange the capsicum across the bottom of the baguette, then top with the tomato, tuna, egg and olives. Drizzle with the remaining dressing, then carefully close the sandwich, ensuring all the filling stays inside the baguette.

5. Wrap the whole baguette in baking paper, then foil, and seal tightly. Store in the fridge until needed. If it's easier to transport in individual portions, cut and wrap before leaving home.

MAKE IT VEG

Omit the tuna and add some grilled haloumi or slices of brie or cheddar in its place.

TIP
Make your sandwiches look more stylish by wrapping them with baking paper tied with rustic twine.

Campfire damper bread three ways

Damper is tried and true campfire bread that pretty much everyone loves, and both kids and adults can get involved in the making. The beer is great for helping the bread rise. I've given a basic damper recipe, along with three different flavour options.

450 g (1 lb/3 cups) self-raising flour, plus about 2–3 tablespoons extra

1 teaspoon salt

2 tablespoons olive oil

250 ml (8½ fl oz/1 cup) beer, at room temperature

Sundried tomato and olive

75 g (2¾ oz/½ cup) chopped sun-dried tomatoes

20–25 pitted kalamata olives, roughly chopped

Cheese and herb

75 g (2¾ oz/¾ cup) grated cheddar or parmesan cheese

3 tablespoons chopped fresh herbs, such as parsley, chives or tarragon, or use 3 teaspoons dried herbs

Pesto

60 g (2 oz/¼ cup) pesto

1. Combine all of the ingredients (reserving about 2 tablespoons of the beer), including your chosen flavouring, in a large bowl (preferably a metal one as it will need to sit by the heat at one point) and use your hands to bring the mixture together. If it's sticky, add a little extra flour. If it's too dry, add the reserved beer. Knead in the bowl for about 10 minutes, or until soft and elastic, then shape it into a ball.

2. Cover the dough with a clean tea towel (dish towel) and place close to the fire (but not on it) or in a warm place for 30 minutes, until the dough has risen in size. At the same time, place your camp oven close to the fire to warm through, but don't let it get too hot.

3. Very lightly dust the base of the camp oven with a little extra flour. Transfer the dough to the camp oven, sprinkle lightly with flour, then cover and sit close to the fire surrounded by coals. Don't sit it on top of the coals or the damper will burn. If cooking over a fire pit with a grill tray that swings around, put the camp oven on this and put some coals on top of the camp oven too, to ensure an all-round heat.

4. Cook for 30–40 minutes, checking the coals every now and then, adding more as necessary, until the damper is cooked and it sounds hollow when tapped. If your damper is taking longer to cook, just keep replacing the coals. Remove from the camp oven, leave for 10 minutes, then serve in chunks or slices.

MAKE AT HOME

Follow the instructions provided, but place the dough in an ovenproof casserole dish or Dutch oven. Bake (with the lid on) at 170°C (340°F) fan-forced for about 40 minutes or until it sounds hollow when tapped on the base.

Goat's cheese, black olive and herb muffins

Makes 12

V

These are best eaten on the day they're made — however, if you do have any left over, warm them up and serve with some butter the next day.

2 free-range eggs, lightly beaten

220 ml (7½ fl oz) milk

1 teaspoon sea salt

150 ml (5 fl oz) olive oil, plus extra for greasing

300 g (10½ oz/2 cups) self-raising flour

120 g (4½ oz/¾ cup) pitted kalamata olives, finely chopped

handful flat-leaf (Italian) parsley, finely chopped

150 g (5½ oz) soft goat's cheese or feta, crumbled

1 red chilli, deseeded and finely chopped (optional)

1. Preheat the oven to 180°C (350°F) fan-forced. Grease a 12-hole (80 ml/2½ fl oz/⅓ cup capacity) muffin tin, or line with cupcake cases.

2. Combine the eggs, milk, salt and olive oil in a bowl. Sift the flour over the egg mixture, then stir gently to combine. Fold in the olives, parsley, cheese and chilli, and season with freshly ground black pepper.

3. Divide the mixture among the muffin holes and bake for 20–25 minutes, or until the muffins have risen and are golden.

4. Leave to cool for 5 minutes in the tin, then transfer to wire racks to cool.

Roasted red capsicum and feta tart

Serves 6

Once you've made and eaten this tart, I wouldn't be surprised if it became one of your regular go-to recipes.

Pastry

230 g (8 oz/1½ cups) plain (all-purpose) flour

100 g (3½ oz) chilled butter, diced

Filling

1 large red capsicum (bell pepper), halved, seeds and membrane removed (or 100 g/3½ oz bought chargrilled capsicum, drained)

3 free-range eggs, lightly beaten

150 ml (5 fl oz) pouring (single/light) cream

100 g (3½ oz) feta cheese, crumbled

Onion jam

2 tablespoons olive oil

2 large onions, thinly sliced

½ teaspoon sea salt

1 tablespoon brown sugar

1 tablespoon balsamic vinegar

1 tablespoon thyme leaves, roughly chopped

1. To make the onion jam, heat the oil in a medium saucepan, add the onion and salt, and stir to coat the onion well. Cover and cook over medium heat for 15 minutes, stirring occasionally, until the onions start to go golden brown. Reduce the heat and cook for a further 15 minutes, still covered. Add the sugar and vinegar, stirring well and scraping up any bits stuck on the bottom of the pan, and cook for another 15 minutes. Stir in the thyme then set aside to cool.

2. Meanwhile, to make the pastry, put the flour into the bowl of a food processor. Add the butter and process for about 30 seconds, or until all the butter is mixed in with the flour and it resembles fine breadcrumbs. Add 50–60 ml (1¾–2 fl oz/2½–3 tablespoons) water and process briefly. Transfer to a bowl and form into a ball. Flatten into a disc, wrap in plastic wrap and chill for 20 minutes.

3. Meanwhile, heat a grill (broiler) to high. Squash the capsicum halves flat, then place under the hot grill, skin side up. Grill until the skin is completely blackened. Place in a plastic bag, seal the bag and leave for 15 minutes. Rub or peel off the skin (do not rinse), then slice the capsicum into thin strips 3–4 cm (1¼–1½ in) long. Set aside.

4. Roll out the pastry and use it to line the base and side of a 23 cm (9 in) flan (tart) tin. Chill for 15 minutes.

5. Preheat the oven to 170°C (340°F) fan-forced. After the pastry has chilled, cover it with baking paper, then weigh down with baking beans or raw rice. Bake for 20 minutes, then remove the paper and weights and bake for a further 5 minutes, or until the base is cooked through. Remove from the oven and set aside.

6. Reduce the oven temperature to 160°C (320°F) fan-forced. Combine the eggs and cream and season well with sea salt and freshly ground black pepper. Spoon the onion jam onto the base of the cooked pastry and sprinkle the feta on top. Pour the egg mixture over the top, to just below the rim of the pastry, then scatter the chargrilled capsicum strips on top.

7. Bake for 20–25 minutes, or until the filling is set and golden, and let it cool in the tin. If transporting, leave the tart whole in the tin to keep it safe. To serve, remove from the tin, then slice.

Italian deli-stuffed loaf

Serves 6

Instead of making six separate sandwiches, make one large filled loaf and then slice it to serve – every slice is packed full of flavoursome ingredients. To save time you could buy the chargrilled vegetables from a deli or supermarket, although I usually prefer to make my own. You could also use an oblong loaf if you can't find a round one.

1 large red capsicum (bell pepper), halved, seeds and membrane removed (or 100 g/3½ oz bought chargrilled capsicum, drained)

1 large zucchini (courgette), halved and thinly sliced lengthways (or 100 g/3½ oz bought chargrilled zucchini, drained)

2 tablespoons olive oil

1 round bread loaf, about 22 cm (9 in) in diameter

1–2 tablespoons pesto

40 g (1½ oz) rocket (arugula)

110 g (4 oz) buffalo mozzarella, sliced

100 g (3½ oz) salami or good-quality ham, thinly sliced

handful basil leaves

1 tablespoon extra virgin olive oil (optional)

MAKE IT VEG

Replace the ham and salami with slices of chargrilled eggplant and some slices of cheddar.

1. Preheat a grill (broiler) to high. Squash the capsicum halves to flatten them, then place under the hot grill, skin side up. Grill until the skin is completely blackened. Place in a plastic bag, seal the bag and leave for 15 minutes. Rub or peel off the skin (do not rinse), then cut the capsicum into 2 cm (¾ in) wide strips and set aside.

2. Meanwhile, heat a chargrill pan over medium heat. Brush the zucchini slices on each side with oil and chargrill until softened.

3. Slice off the top of the loaf, about 3 cm (1¼ in) from the top, and reserve this to use as a lid. Hollow out the loaf, leaving about a 2 cm (¾ in) border all the way around. (You can use the scooped-out bread to make breadcrumbs.)

4. Brush the entire inside of the bread and the bottom of the lid with pesto, and season with sea salt and freshly ground black pepper. Place the rocket in the base, then top with the zucchini, making an even layer. Top with the mozzarella, then the salami, and next the capsicum. Scatter over the basil leaves, and drizzle the olive oil on top, if you like. Cover with the lid.

5. Wrap the loaf in plastic wrap and put on a plate. Place a second plate on top and put a tin or two on top of the plate to weigh it down slightly. Leave in the fridge for 1 hour, or up to 4 hours, to allow the flavours to develop.

6. Wrap the loaf in a clean tea towel (dish towel) to transport it, and slice into thick wedges to serve.

Chicken and pork picnic pot pie

Serves 8–10

This is a rich savoury pie, the kind we used to take on picnics in England. It's made up of layers of poached chicken, sausage meat and a bacon-and-sweet-corn stuffing, all encased in a delicious shortcrust pastry. For added flavour, I use sausage meat from sausages, rather than plain sausage meat. If using sausages, don't worry too much about the amount - anywhere from 400–500 g will work just fine for this recipe.

500 g (1 lb 2 oz) boneless, skinless chicken breasts,

450 g (14 oz–1 lb 2 oz) good-quality pork sausages

1 free-range egg, beaten

green salad, to serve

chutney, to serve

Pastry

400 g (14 oz/2⅔ cups) plain (all-purpose) flour

180 g (6½ oz) chilled butter, diced

Stuffing

2 teaspoons olive oil

75 g (2¾ oz) rindless bacon, roughly chopped

1 small onion, finely chopped

2 garlic cloves, crushed

100 g (3½ oz/1¼ cups) fresh breadcrumbs (from day-old bread)

handful flat-leaf (Italian) parsley, chopped

handful basil, chopped

1 corn cob, kernels sliced off (or 100 g/3½ oz frozen corn, thawed)

1 free-range egg, beaten

25 g (1 oz) butter, melted

1. To make the pastry, put the flour and butter into a food processor and mix for about 30 seconds, until the mixture resembles fine breadcrumbs. Add 100 ml (3½ fl oz) cold water and process for 10 seconds. Transfer to a large bowl or work surface and form into a ball, adding a little more water if necessary, and knead very briefly. Divide the pastry into two portions of about ⅓ and ⅔. Press each portion into a disc and wrap in plastic wrap. Chill for 15 minutes.

2. Roll out the larger of the two pastry pieces to a circle about 33 cm (13 in), or sufficient to line the base and side of a 20 cm (8 in) springform or loose-based pie tin about 6 cm (2⅓ in) deep, allowing any excess pastry to hang over the sides. Chill until needed.

3. Slice the chicken breasts in half horizontally. Place in a saucepan and add just enough water to cover the chicken. Bring to the boil, then reduce the heat to a simmer and cook for 5 minutes. Remove from the heat and leave for 10 minutes (the chicken doesn't have to be cooked through). Drain the water and set aside.

4. To make the stuffing, heat the oil in a frying pan and fry the bacon for 3 minutes. Add the onion and garlic and fry for about 5 minutes, until softened. Transfer to a bowl and leave in the water to cool for 5 minutes. Stir in the breadcrumbs, parsley, basil, corn and beaten egg. Mix thoroughly, season well with sea salt and freshly ground black pepper and stir in the melted butter.

5. Preheat the oven to 180°C (350°F) fan-forced. Take half the stuffing and spread it over the pastry base, pressing it down gently with the back of a spoon. Shred the chicken and layer it on top.

6. Slit the skins of the sausages and put the meat into a bowl, squashing it all together, then spread it in a layer over the chicken, pressing it out to the edges. Top with the remaining stuffing, once again gently pressing it down.

7. Roll out the remaining pastry to a circle about 22 cm (8½ in) across, or enough to cover the dish. Brush the top edge of the overhanging pastry in the tin with the beaten egg, then lift the pastry lid onto the pie. Seal together gently, pressing down with the tines of a fork. Trim the edges, ensuring the pie is well sealed. Brush the lid with beaten egg, then cut a cross in the middle to allow steam to escape.

8. Place the pie on a baking tray and bake for 50 minutes. Brush the top with egg again, to give a glossy finish, and bake for a further 10 minutes. Leave to cool completely in the tin before slicing. If transporting the pie, leave it in the tin to keep it safe. Serve with a dressed green salad and chutney.

Coronation chicken baguettes with crunchy apple slaw

Serves 4–6

Coronation chicken is a dish that's often joked about as being old-fashioned, but I doubt you'll get any complaints with this version, served in a crusty baguette with crunchy apple slaw. This recipe makes sufficient filling for a baguette that's about 60 cm (24 in) long. You could also use a couple of ciabatta loaves.

35 g (1¼ oz/⅓ cup) flaked almonds

80 g (2¾ oz) good-quality egg mayonnaise

2 tablespoons sour cream

2 teaspoons Indian curry paste, or 1 teaspoon curry powder

2 teaspoons tomato paste (concentrated purée)

1 tablespoon lemon juice

3 tablespoons mango or apricot chutney

300–350 g (10½ oz–12½ oz) cooked chicken, preferably free-range, shredded

1 sourdough baguette, about 60 cm (24 in)

Crunchy apple slaw

1 green apple, halved, cored and cut into thin matchsticks

1½ tablespoons lemon juice

150 g (5½ oz) white cabbage, core removed, finely shredded

handful coriander (cilantro) leaves, roughly torn

1 tablespoon olive oil

1. Heat a frying pan over medium heat. Add the almonds and toast for a few minutes until golden, shaking the pan regularly. Set aside to cool.

2. Whisk together the mayonnaise, sour cream, curry paste, tomato paste, lemon juice and chutney, then season with sea salt and freshly ground black pepper. Gently stir the chicken and almonds into the mayonnaise dressing.

3. To make the slaw, put the apple in a bowl, add 2 teaspoons of the lemon juice and toss to coat to stop them oxidising. Add the cabbage and coriander. Combine the oil and remaining lemon juice and season with salt and pepper. Add to the apple mixture and toss gently to combine.

4. Cut open the baguette most of the way through, but leaving enough to keep the two sides together. Divide the apple slaw among the baguette pieces, then top with the chicken mixture. Wrap in baking paper, twisting the ends to secure.

5. Store in the fridge until needed, and transport in a cool box.

Roasted pumpkin, parmesan and herb pasties

These pasties are so delicious that one is rarely enough! For convenience they can be frozen uncooked, and then baked as required. If cooking from frozen, bake for an additional 5 minutes.

1 whole garlic bulb

2 tablespoons olive oil

300 g (10½ oz) pumpkin (winter squash) peeled and cut into approximately 1.5 cm (½ in) cubes

75 g (2¾ oz/¾ cup) grated parmesan cheese

2 tablespoons finely chopped flat-leaf (Italian) parsley

2 tablespoons shredded basil

3 sheets frozen puff pastry, about 24 × 24 cm (9½ × 9½ in), thawed in fridge

1 free-range egg, lightly beaten

1 tablespoon milk

1 tablespoon sesame or poppy seeds (optional)

chutney, to serve (optional)

1. Preheat the oven to 180°C (350°F) fan-forced. Wrap the garlic bulb in foil and place on a baking sheet. Roast for 50–60 minutes, or until it feels very soft.

2. While the garlic is in the oven, roast the pumpkin as well. Add the oil to a roasting tin and heat in the oven for 10 minutes. Add the pumpkin, season with sea salt and freshly ground black pepper and roast for 25–30 minutes, or until it is soft and a few of the corners are starting to blacken. Set aside for 10 minutes to cool, leaving the oven turned on.

3. When cool enough to handle, snip the tops off the garlic cloves, then squeeze the purée from each clove into a bowl. Add the parmesan, parsley and basil and season with salt and pepper. Add the cooled pumpkin and any pan juices and mix to combine.

4. Cut out four 10 cm (4 in) circles from each sheet of pastry. Divide the pumpkin mixture among the circles, placing it onto one half of each circle only.

5. Combine the egg and milk, then brush the edges of the pastry. Fold the pastry over and gently seal, then press along the edges with the tines of a fork. Brush all over with the egg mixture and sprinkle with sesame seeds, if using. Place on two or three lined baking sheets and bake for 20–25 minutes, or until the pasties are puffed and golden. Serve warm or at room temperature, with a small bowl of chutney, if desired.

Fire up the

barbecue

Vietnamese pork meatballs with noodles

These meatballs are quick and easy to make and can also be served on their own, without the noodles and dressing. Sometimes I make big ones, but at other times, particularly if I'm feeding a crowd, I make them half the size.

Meatballs

800 g (1 lb 12 oz) minced pork

1 small red chilli, deseeded and finely chopped (optional)

3 garlic cloves, crushed

1½ tablespoons fish sauce

handful mint leaves, finely chopped

handful coriander (cilantro) leaves, finely chopped

250 g (9 oz) rice vermicelli noodles, to serve

Vietnamese dressing

2 tablespoons fish sauce

½ small red chilli, deseeded and finely chopped

1½ tablespoons lime juice

1 teaspoon sugar

1. Put all of the meatball ingredients into a bowl, season well with salt and freshly ground black pepper and use your hands to mix well until the pork turns a paler pink. Taking a tablespoon of the mixture at a time, roll into neat balls – about 16 in total. Alternatively, take 2 teaspoons at a time to make 32 smaller balls. These can be made in advance and chilled in a cool box.

2. To make the Vietnamese dressing, put all of the ingredients into a small bowl and stir to dissolve the sugar. Set aside.

3. Cook the meatballs on a medium–hot barbecue or on a grill rack over a fire for 10–12 minutes for the larger meatballs, or 8–9 minutes for the smaller ones, turning regularly, until just cooked through. Be careful not to overcook, otherwise they will become dry.

4. Meanwhile, cook the noodles in boiling water for 2 minutes, or according to the packet instructions. Drain and rinse in cold water to cool. To serve, pour the dressing over the noodles and toss to combine, then sit the meatballs on top. Alternatively, serve the meatballs, noodles and dressing separately, allowing each person to help themselves.

Marinated butterflied leg of lamb

If you're taking this camping or to a barbecue away from home, you could marinate the lamb beforehand, not only saving time but also adding some extra flavour. You could also do this even if you're cooking it at home. If you have any leftovers, a lamb and chutney sandwich will win hearts the next day!

2–2.5 kg (4 lb 6½ oz–5 lb 8 oz) (a little less without the bone) leg of lamb, boned and butterflied

80 ml (2½ fl oz/⅓ cup) olive oil

juice of 1 lemon, (plus 1-2 lemons, halved, optional)

1 teaspoon ground coriander

1 teaspoon ground cumin

2 teaspoons dried mint

2 garlic cloves, crushed

green salad, to serve

baked potatoes or potato salad, to serve

small handful flat-leaf (Italian) parsley leaves

1 small red chilli, thinly sliced, seeds removed if preferred

1. Open the lamb out and use a sharp knife to make a few slashes through the thickest part of the meat – this helps the meat cook evenly.

2. In a bowl, combine the olive oil, lemon juice, coriander, cumin, mint and garlic. Rub the marinade all over the lamb. If possible, return the meat to the fridge or a cool box (place it on a tray or even in a clean plastic bag) and leave to marinate for 1–2 hours. Ideally you would prepare this in the morning and allow it to marinate all day.

3. When you're ready to cook, ensure your barbecue or fire isn't too hot, otherwise your meat will char on the outside and still be raw in the middle. Cook the meat for 15 minutes, then turn over and cook for a further 15 minutes. If you are cooking on a hooded barbecue put the hood down for the second 15 minutes. If not, try and cover your meat with foil. If you can't do either, don't worry.

4. Check to see if the meat is cooked to your liking, remembering it will cook further while it rests. If it's ready, remove from the heat, wrap in foil and leave to rest for about 10 minutes. While the meat is resting, char the lemon halves (if using), cut side down on the barbecue for 2-3 mins. Slice the lamb, scatter over the parsley and chilli and serve with salad and baked potatoes.

TIP
If you're going camping, get the butcher to vacuum bag the lamb to keep it fresh for a few extra days. You can also combine the coriander, cumin and mint in a small jar before you leave home and add to the remaining ingredients before cooking to avoid bringing multiple jars.

TIP

Balsamic onion relish can be served warm or cool. It works well served as an accompaniment to chargrilled steak and chicken, or is equally at home on cheese or chicken sandwiches. Any leftovers can be covered and stored in the cool box for up to two days.

Pesto lamb burgers

Nearly everyone loves a good burger and homemade or camp-made are best. These are so simple the kids can get involved too. This recipe makes four large burgers, but you could easily make eight smaller ones, if preferred. The pesto flavour is quite mild, so add the extra tablespoon if you really love it.

4 burger buns or soft rolls (8 if making smaller burgers), to serve

crisp lettuce leaves, to serve

tomato, sliced, to serve

cucumber, sliced, to serve

mayonnaise, to serve (optional)

Pesto lamb patties

800 g (1 lb 12 oz) minced lamb

2 garlic cloves, crushed

2–3 tablespoons pesto

Quick balsamic onion relish

2 onions, halved and thinly sliced

1 tablespoon olive oil

1 tablespoon balsamic vinegar

2 teaspoons sugar

1. Put the lamb, garlic and pesto into a large bowl and season with salt and freshly ground black pepper. Use your hands to combine well.

2. Divide the lamb mixture into 4 portions (or 8 if making smaller burgers), then shape into patties. The burgers can be prepared ahead and stored in a cool box, if desired.

3. To make the onion relish, place the onion in a bowl, add the oil and toss to coat. Place onto a hot barbecue flatplate or in a frying pan over a fire or gas cooker and cook for about 10 minutes, stirring regularly so they soften and turn golden brown but don't burn.

4. Scoop the onion into a pile, pour over the vinegar and sprinkle over the sugar. Mix together using a fork or tongs and cook for a further 6–8 minutes.

5. Cook the patties on a barbecue or on a grill rack over a fire for about 6 minutes on each side, or 4–5 minutes on each side if making smaller burgers.

6. To assemble the burgers, split the burger buns or rolls and toast them, cut side down, for 1–2 minutes to warm through. Spread with mayonnaise, if desired.

7. Serve each burger inside a bun with as much lettuce, tomato and cucumber as desired, then top with the balsamic onion relish.

Marinated pork loin with Greek salad

Serves 4–6

Pork loin (fillet) is a fairly quick-cooking meat, but be careful that you don't burn the outside before the inside is sufficiently cooked. It is important to rest the meat afterwards so it can finish cooking.

60 ml (2 fl oz/¼ cup) olive oil

2 tablespoons lemon juice

2 teaspoons dried oregano

2 pork fillets (about 800 g/ 1 lb 12 oz)

pita bread, to serve (optional)

Greek salad

½ small red onion, thinly sliced

3 tomatoes, roughly chopped

2 Lebanese (short) cucumbers, diced

150 g (5½ oz) black olives

200 g (7 oz) feta cheese

olive oil, for drizzling

1. Combine the olive oil, lemon juice and oregano in a shallow dish and season with salt and freshly ground black pepper.

2. Cut several shallow slashes across both sides of the pork to allow the marinade to get into the meat. Put the meat into the dish and turn in the marinade a few times to coat. Set aside in the fridge or a cool box for at least 2 hours to marinate.

3. Remove the pork from the marinade and, if possible, pat dry with paper towel – this helps to get the outside nice and crisp.

4. Cook the pork on a barbecue or grill rack over a fire for 3–4 minutes on each side. If possible, wrap the meat in foil (to prevent the outside burning before the middle is cooked), then move to a cooler part of the barbecue or to the side of the fire and continue cooking for about 15 minutes – it is safe to serve the meat when it is still a little pink in the middle.

5. Once cooked, let the foil-wrapped pork rest for about 10 minutes – this is important for it to finish cooking. If you didn't wrap it during cooking then cover the pork with a bowl while resting.

6. If serving with pita bread, place them over the heat briefly, turning once, until lightly toasted and warmed through.

7. While the pork is resting, make the Greek salad. Combine the onion, tomato, cucumber and olives in a serving bowl. Crumble the feta cheese on top and drizzle with olive oil. Slice the pork and serve with the salad and pita bread, if desired.

TIP

This recipe also works really well with a teriyaki marinade. Combine 80 ml (2½ fl oz/⅓ cup) soy sauce, 80 ml (2½ fl oz/⅓ cup) mirin, 1 teaspoon sesame oil and 2 tablespoons honey in a large shallow dish and stir well to combine. Add a crushed garlic clove and season with pepper.

Pork kebabs with flavoured mayonnaise

It's up to you how you flavour the mayonnaise, you can add your favourite fresh herbs, a little chilli, a squeeze of lemon juice, a dollop of mustard, or experiment with a combination to find the right mix for you! Buy the best quality egg mayonnaise you can find.

2 tablespoons hoisin sauce

2 tablespoons soy sauce

450–500 g (1 lb–1 lb 2 oz) pork fillet, cut into about 24 cubes

16 small brown mushrooms

2 small zucchini (courgettes), cut into 1 cm (⅓ in) slices

1 red capsicum (bell pepper), seeds and membrane removed, cut into 3 cm (1¼ in) squares

olive or vegetable oil, for brushing

salad and pita bread, to serve (optional)

Mustard and herb mayonnaise

120 g (4½ oz/½ cup) egg mayonnaise

1 tablespoon lemon juice

1 tablespoon finely chopped fresh herbs, such as parsley, coriander (cilantro), tarragon or dill

1 tablespoon dijon or wholegrain mustard

1 small red chilli, deseeded and finely chopped (optional)

1. If using wooden skewers, soak 8 of them in water for 20 minutes to prevent them from burning during cooking.

2. Combine the hoisin and soy sauces in a medium-sized bowl and season with freshly ground black pepper. Add the pork and toss to coat. Cover and leave to marinate in the fridge or a cool box for at least 1 hour if you have time; if not they will still taste delicious.

3. Meanwhile, make the mustard and herb mayonnaise. Combine the mayonnaise with your choice of ingredients in a small bowl. Stir in 1 teaspoon water and set aside. If you're not adding lemon juice, add a couple more teaspoons of water.

4. Alternately thread the pork and vegetables onto the skewers. Pour any remaining marinade over the vegetables. Brush or drizzle each kebab with oil.

5. Preheat a barbecue grill plate to medium and cook the kebabs for about 10 minutes, turning regularly, or until the pork is cooked.

6. Serve the kebabs with the mustard and herb mayonnaise and a salad, if desired. If serving as a wrap, cover the pita bread in foil and warm on the barbecue for about 5 minutes before serving. Pull the pork and vegetables from the skewers and add to the pitas along with a dollop of the mayonnaise.

MAKE IT VEG

Replace the pork with cubes of haloumi and/or cherry tomatoes and cook for 2–3 mins on each side.

Marinated fish fillets

Serves 4

This tasty marinade relies on fresh coriander and a mixture of spices for its delicious flavour – you can make it in advance or on location. If you've got a fire going, wrap some potatoes in foil and bake for 45–60 minutes in the hot coals to serve alongside the fish for a memorable fireside dinner.

1 teaspoon ground coriander

1 teaspoon ground cumin

1 teaspoon ground ginger

2 tablespoons olive oil

2 garlic cloves, crushed

1 teaspoon harissa paste

2 tablespoons chopped coriander (cilantro) leaves

4 × 180–200 g (6½–7 oz) salmon, cod, snapper or other firm fish fillets

1. Heat a small frying pan over medium heat. Add the ground coriander, cumin and ginger and dry-roast for about 1 minute, shaking the pan regularly. Transfer to a small bowl.

2. Add the oil, garlic, harissa and coriander leaves to the bowl with the spices, season with salt and freshly ground black pepper, and mix well.

3. Put the fish fillets into a shallow dish (or resealable bag if making this on location) and add the marinade. Massage the fish gently to coat. Place in the fridge or a cool box for a couple of hours to allow the flavours to penetrate.

4. Cook the fish in a pan over medium–high heat for about 5 minutes on each side, or cook it on a gas cooker, barbecue or on a grill rack over a fire if cooking on location. If the fire is very hot, sit the fish at the edge, otherwise the outside will burn before the inside is cooked. Cooking times will depend on the thickness of your fish. Do not overcook the fish, or it will be dry.

One-pot

camping
dishes

Easy fish and vegetable stew

Serves 4

You can use almost any fresh fish for this stew, although avoid using oily fish such as mackerel. The sugar is used to counterbalance the acidity of the wine and tomatoes, but isn't vital. You can also add carrots to this stew if you have some. Roughly chop and add them at the same time as the potatoes.

2 tablespoons olive oil

1 onion, halved and thinly sliced

2 garlic cloves, crushed

12 small waxy potatoes, quartered

250 ml (8½ fl oz/1 cup) white wine

400 g (14 oz) tin diced tomatoes

600 g (1 lb 5 oz) skinless, boneless fish fillets, cut into bite-sized pieces

1 handful green beans, trimmed and cut into 3 cm (1¼ in) lengths

2 teaspoons sugar (optional)

1. Heat the oil in a camp oven or large heavy-based frying pan over a fire or gas cooker. Add the onion and garlic, cover, and cook for 5–10 minutes, stirring regularly until lightly golden. Season with salt and pepper.

2. Add the potatoes and cook for a couple of minutes. Pour in the wine and let it boil for a minute or two, scraping the base of the pan with a wooden spoon.

3. Add the tomatoes and about 125 ml (½ cup) water, or just enough to ensure the potatoes are submerged. Cover with a lid and move the camp oven to the side of the fire, with a few coals underneath and some coals around the base of the camp oven. Simmer for about 25 minutes, or until the potatoes are tender when pierced with a fork.

4. Add the fish, beans and sugar, if using, and season with salt and freshly ground black pepper. Cover and cook for a further 5 minutes, or until the beans are tender and the fish is cooked.

5. Divide the fish stew among bowls and serve immediately.

MAKE AT HOME

Follow the instructions above, but use a large casserole dish or saucepan over medium–high heat, and turn the heat down to low to simmer.

One-pot lamb shoulder with white beans and tomato sauce

Serves 4–6

There are a couple of optional ingredients in this recipe, it's up to you if you want to add them. The feta is a salty, creamy addition that softens the tomato sauce flavour, while the olives are there just because I love black olives!

2 tablespoons olive oil

1 large onion, halved and sliced

2 garlic cloves, chopped

1.2–1.4 kg (2 lb 10 oz–3 lb 1 oz) boneless shoulder of lamb

375 ml (12½ fl oz/1½ cups) red wine

2 × 400 g (14 oz) tins diced tomatoes

1 teaspoon dried oregano

2 × 400 g (14 oz) tins cannellini beans, drained and rinsed

about 20 pitted kalamata olives (optional)

200 g (7 oz) feta cheese, crumbled, to serve (optional)

crusty bread or damper (see page 22), to serve

steamed green beans or other vegetables, to serve

1. Heat the oil in a camp oven or large heavy-based saucepan on a grill rack over a fire. Add the onion and garlic and cook for about 10 minutes, stirring regularly, or until lightly golden.

2. Add the lamb and cook for about 10 minutes, turning the lamb to brown on all sides. Add the red wine, tomatoes and oregano. Season with salt and freshly ground black pepper, cover, and bring to the boil.

3. Move the camp oven to the side of the fire, with a few coals underneath. Place coals on the lid and place coals around the base of the camp oven, and cook for 2 hours. Replenish the coals every 30 minutes or so to ensure it keeps cooking. Check the dish occasionally, making sure there is still plenty of sauce – if not add a little extra water. If cooking on the side of the fire, turn the camp oven every 15 minutes to ensure it keeps simmering gently and cooks evenly.

4. Add the cannellini beans and olives, if using, and cook for a further 30 minutes, or until the lamb is very tender.

5. Using two forks (with the lamb still in the pan), shred the meat into bite-sized pieces and stir into the sauce. Scatter over the feta, if using, and divide among bowls. Serve with crusty bread or damper and steamed greens.

MAKE AT HOME

Follow the instructions above, but use a large ovenproof casserole dish over medium–high heat. After bringing to the boil, cook, covered, in a preheated oven (160°C/320°F fan-forced) for 2 hours. Add the beans and olives and cook for another 30 minutes.

One-pot roast chicken with vegetables

Serves 4

This dish couldn't really be any simpler – chop your vegetables, put them in a casserole dish, top with a whole chicken, then leave it to cook over the fire while you sit back and enjoy the afternoon. If you're anything like my family, it will give you the chance to play a spontaneous game of cricket. When the game is over, dinner for your ravenous team is ready and waiting.

80 ml (2½ fl oz/⅓ cup) olive oil or vegetable oil

3 large floury potatoes, cut into 3 cm (1¼ in) chunks

4 carrots, cut into 3 cm (1¼ in) chunks

1 red onion, cut into 8 wedges

4 garlic cloves, peeled and squashed with the back of a blunt knife

1.5 kg (3 lb 5 oz) whole chicken, preferably free-range

steamed green vegetables or a salad, to serve (optional)

1. Heat 60 ml (2 fl oz/¼ cup) of the oil in a large camp oven or casserole dish on a grill rack over a fire. Once the oil is hot, add the potato, carrot, onion and two of the garlic cloves. Season with salt and freshly ground black pepper and stir to coat the vegetables in the oil.

2. Put the remaining squashed garlic inside the chicken, then drizzle or brush the outside of the chicken with the remaining oil and season with salt and pepper. Use a sharp knife to make two slits in each thigh to help it cook evenly.

3. Sit the chicken among the vegetables, moving the vegetables to surround it if necessary, and cover with a lid. Move the camp oven to the side of the fire, with a few coals underneath. Place coals on the lid and around the base of the camp oven, and cook for 1½–2 hours, or until the vegetables and chicken are tender. You will need to stir occasionally to prevent the vegetables on the bottom from burning. Check the chicken is ready by piercing the thigh, the juices will run clear when cooked.

4. Remove from the fire and let it sit, covered, for 5 minutes. Carefully remove the chicken, tipping any juices back into the dish. Carve the chicken and serve with the vegetables and steamed greens or a salad on the side.

MAKE AT HOME

Follow the instructions above, but instead use a large casserole dish. Cook in a preheated oven (200°C/400°F fan-forced) for about 1¼ hours. Then remove the lid and cook for a further 15–20 minutes to brown the top, or until the chicken is cooked through.

TIP
Do not expect the chicken to go golden brown while cooking. However, you will end up with a very tender, moist chicken.

TIP

A couple of chopped bacon slices thrown in with the onion makes a tasty addition to this dish.

Hearty bean and vegetable 'stoup'

Serves 4

V

We go camping throughout winter as well as summer, although I have to admit that even we draw the line at camping when we know it's going to rain. This dish is brilliant whatever the weather – the name says it all really – it is a cross between a stew and a soup, hence the name our family has given to this 'stoup'!

2 tablespoons olive oil or vegetable oil

1 onion, chopped

2 garlic cloves, roughly chopped

1 large leek, sliced

2 carrots, peeled and sliced

3 large potatoes, cut into small chunks

400 g (14 oz) tin cannellini or borlotti beans, rinsed and drained

400 g (14 oz) tin diced tomatoes

crusty bread or damper (*see* page 22), to serve

grated parmesan, cheddar or tasty cheese, to serve (optional)

1. Heat the oil in a large saucepan or camp oven on a grill rack over a fire or on a gas cooker. Add the onion, garlic and leek and cook, stirring regularly, for about 10 minutes. If it gets too hot, add a dash of water to the pan to cool it down.

2. Add the carrot and potato to the pan and stir well to combine. Add the beans and tomatoes, then add 1½ tins of water (using the tomato tin) and stir gently. Season with salt and freshly ground black pepper, ensure all the vegetables are submerged, then cover and return to the boil.

3. Once boiling, move the camp oven to the side of the fire, with a few coals underneath. Then place coals around the base of the camp oven and cook for about 35 minutes, or until the vegetables are tender. You may need to replace the coals every so often to keep it simmering. It's okay to let this dish sit for a while – it will become a bit mushy but the flavour will be great.

4. Check the seasoning and adjust as desired, then divide the soup among bowls and serve with crusty bread or damper. It also tastes great with a little grated cheese on top.

MAKE AT HOME

Follow the instructions above, but use a large casserole dish or saucepan. Cook over medium–high heat. After bringing to the boil, turn the heat down to low and cook, covered, for about 35 minutes, or until the vegetables are tender.

Vegetable and chickpea casserole

This dish is reminiscent of a French-style ratatouille, but with extra vegetables and chickpeas. It can be served as a main meal with couscous or as a side to grilled meat and fish. Alternatively, for a quick meal, serve hot or cold with slices of crusty bread.

60 ml (2 fl oz/¼ cup) olive oil

1 large onion, halved and thinly sliced

1 red capsicum (bell pepper), seeds and membranes removed, cut into thin strips

2 garlic cloves, crushed

2 eggplants (aubergines), halved lengthways and cut into 1 cm (⅓ in) slices

2 zucchini (courgettes), cut into 1 cm (⅓ in) slices

400 g (14 oz) tin diced tomatoes

400 g (14 oz) tin chickpeas, rinsed and drained

½ teaspoon ground coriander

1 small handful basil leaves, roughly torn

grated parmesan cheese, to serve

1. Heat 2 tablespoons of the oil in a camp oven on a grill rack over a fire or a large heavy-based casserole dish or saucepan over medium heat. Add the onion and cook for about 5 minutes, or until soft.

2. Add the capsicum, garlic, eggplant, zucchini and remaining tablespoon of oil. Stir well and cover. Continue to cook on the rack, but move the camp oven away from direct heat. Cook for 25–30 minutes, stirring occasionally. Keep an eye on the heat level: it needs to be hot enough to keep cooking but not so hot it dries out.

3. Add the tomatoes, chickpeas and coriander. Season with salt and freshly ground black pepper, cover again, and simmer for a further 20 minutes, or until the vegetables are soft but not mushy.

4. Stir in the basil. Serve with parmesan scattered over the top, if desired.

MAKE AT HOME

Follow the instructions above, but use a large casserole dish or saucepan. Cook over medium–high heat, and turn the heat down to low when covering the dish.

Beef, mushroom, potato and red wine casserole

Serves 4–6

You can make life at the campsite a bit easier by putting the flour and cumin in a large resealable bag before you leave home. Then, when you come to cook dinner at the campsite, you just need to put the cubes of meat into the bag and shake it in the pre-seasoned flour. This recipe can easily be doubled to serve more if you're camping with several families, just make sure you have a big enough pot to cook it in!

60 ml (2 fl oz/¼ cup) olive oil or vegetable oil

2 onions, chopped

3 garlic cloves, crushed

2–3 carrots, peeled and sliced

2 tablespoons plain (all-purpose) flour

½ teaspoon ground cumin

800 g–1 kg (1 lb 12 oz– 2 lb 3 oz) cubed beef blade steak

250 ml (8½ fl oz/1 cup) red wine

400 g (14 oz) tin diced tomatoes

3–4 large potatoes, roughly chopped

3–4 field mushrooms, roughly chopped

1. Heat the oil in a large camp oven or casserole dish on a grill rack over a fire. Add the onion and garlic and cook for 10 minutes, stirring regularly, until softened.

2. Meanwhile, put the flour and cumin in a resealable bag or clean plastic bag and season with salt and freshly ground black pepper. Add the meat and shake it well to coat the beef cubes. Add the meat to the dish, making sure it is on the hot part of the fire, stirring for a few minutes until the meat is light brown on all sides.

3. Add the wine to the dish and bring to the boil, stir using a wooden spoon to scrape any bits stuck to the base of the dish. Cook for 1 minute, then add the carrots, tomatoes and ½ a tin of water (use the tomato tin) and move to a cooler part of the fire away from direct heat. Cover and simmer gently for about 20 minutes, or until the potatoes are tender.

4. Add the potatoes and mushrooms to the dish and cook for 50 minutes. Stir everything around and let the potatoes break down in the sauce.

5. Remove from the fire and set aside for 5 minutes. Adjust the seasoning as necessary, then divide the casserole among bowls and serve.

MAKE AT HOME

Follow the instructions above, but use a large casserole dish and cook in a preheated oven (170°C/340°F fan-forced).

Salads

big &

small

Chargrilled lamb with haloumi, olives and lemon

Serves 4

Drawing on the flavours of Greece, this salad is always popular, and cooking the lamb over a fire gives it a delicious smoky flavour. Ask your butcher to bone out a loin of lamb to give you backstrap and fillet. This is much cheaper than just asking for lamb fillet or buying it at the supermarket. One lemon should provide enough juice for the lamb and the dressing.

1 tablespoon olive oil

2 garlic cloves, crushed

1 teaspoon dried oregano

1 tablespoon lemon juice

600 g (1 lb 5 oz) lamb fillet

3 tomatoes, roughly chopped

16 pitted kalamata olives

2 tablespoons capers, roughly chopped

large handful of rocket (arugula) (optional)

250 g (9 oz) haloumi cheese, cut into 1 cm (½ in) thick slices widthways

crusty bread or damper (see page 22), to serve

Lemon and herb dressing

2 tablespoons olive oil

1 tablespoon lemon juice

1 teaspoon dried oregano

1. Combine the olive oil, garlic, oregano and lemon juice in a shallow container, and season with sea salt and freshly ground black pepper. Add the lamb and turn to coat in the marinade. Set aside in the fridge or a cool box for 30 minutes. This isn't essential, but it will enhance the flavour.

2. Remove the lamb from the marinade (reserving the marinade) and pat the lamb dry with paper towel.

3. Cook the lamb on a chargrill pan or barbecue hotplate over high heat for about 2 minutes on each side, or until seared on the outside and medium–rare on the inside. The exact timing will depend on the thickness of the meat. Set aside to rest for 5 minutes, then cut the lamb into thin slices.

4. Combine the lamb, tomato, olives, capers and rocket, if using, in a large bowl. Combine the lemon and herb dressing ingredients in a separate small bowl and drizzle over the lamb, tossing to combine.

5. Dunk both sides of the haloumi into the reserved marinade. Cook for 1–2 minutes on each side until golden.

6. Top the salad with the haloumi and serve soon after cooking, or the haloumi will become rubbery. Serve with crusty bread for mopping up all the delicious juices.

Pasta salad with bacon, avocado, rocket and cherry tomatoes

Serves 4

This is a great way to use up any leftover cooked pasta. Different pasta shapes can be combined together, so you can use up any packets you may have lying around that haven't been finished off. If you know you're going to be making this for lunch or dinner, cook extra bacon at breakfast and store it in the fridge or a cool box until needed.

600–700 g (1 lb 5 oz– 1 lb 9 oz) cold cooked pasta (or 300 g/10½ oz) dried pasta cooked, drained and cooled)

6 bacon slices, cooked until crisp, then roughly chopped

2 avocados, diced

250 g (9 oz) cherry tomatoes, quartered

2 handfuls rocket (arugula) or other salad leaves

Balsamic chilli dressing

60 ml (2 fl oz/¼ cup) olive oil

1 tablespoon balsamic or white wine vinegar

1 red chilli, deseeded and finely diced

1. Put the cooked pasta in a large bowl. Add the bacon, avocado, tomato and rocket and mix well.

2. Combine all the dressing ingredients in a small bowl and season with salt and freshly ground black pepper. Pour over the salad and toss to coat – if you have time, leave for about 20 minutes to allow all the flavours to mingle before serving.

MAKE IT VEG

Omit the bacon and add vegan parmesan to make this vegan.

Chargrilled zucchini, onion and feta salad

I love chargilled vegetables, so if we've got a fire or barbecue going, I always like to throw some on, then I think about what else I can add to create a complete meal – they're great served alongside meat or fish dishes. The salad leaves are entirely optional, add some if you have any available.

80 ml (2½ fl oz/⅓ cup) olive oil

2 tablespoon balsamic vinegar

3 zucchini (courgettes), cut lengthways into 1 cm (⅓ in) slices

2 red or brown onions, cut into thin wedges

1 teaspoon dried oregano

large handful salad leaves or rocket (arugula) (optional)

200 g (7 oz) feta cheese, crumbled

MAKE IT VEG

Use non-dairy/vegan cheese to make this vegan.

1. To make the dressing, combine the olive oil and balsamic vinegar in a small bowl and season well with salt and freshly ground black pepper.

2. Put the zucchini on a plate and spoon over about 1 tablespoon of the dressing, turn to coat, then place on a medium–hot barbecue flatplate or grill rack over a fire. Repeat with the onion wedges and place over the heat. Cook the vegetables for 8–10 minutes, turning regularly until softened and starting to blacken.

3. Remove the vegetables from the heat and set aside to cool. Meanwhile, whisk the oregano into the remaining dressing.

4. Once the vegetables have cooled, toss together with the salad leaves, if using. Scatter the feta over the vegetables, drizzle with the dressing and serve.

Quinoa salad with goat's cheese, basil and crisp prosciutto

Serves 4

This is a rich, indulgent salad, full of big flavours. You can replace the goat's cheese with feta or a more mildly flavoured bocconcini (fresh baby mozzarella) if you prefer.

150 g (5½ oz/¾ cup) quinoa

60 ml (2 fl oz/¼ cup) olive oil

2 tablespoons sherry vinegar or white wine vinegar

3 tablespoons small capers, rinsed and finely chopped

100 g (3½ oz) prosciutto

handful basil leaves, larger leaves roughly torn

½ bunch watercress, leaves picked, or 80 g (2¾ oz) rocket or other salad leaves

150 g (5½ oz) goat's cheese, broken into small pieces

MAKE IT VEG

Replace the prosciutto with chopped avocado.

1. Bring 375 ml (12½ fl oz/1½ cups) water to the boil in a medium saucepan. Add the quinoa, cover and return to the boil. Reduce the heat and simmer, covered, for 15 minutes, or until all the water has been absorbed. Remove from the heat and place a clean tea towel (dish towel) over the saucepan, putting the lid on top of the tea towel; this helps any remaining moisture to be absorbed. Leave for 10 minutes.

2. Put the quinoa in a bowl and add 2 tablespoons of the oil and the vinegar and capers. Season well with sea salt and freshly ground black pepper. Toss to combine, then set aside to cool to room temperature.

3. Heat the remaining tablespoon of oil in a frying pan over medium–high heat. Add the prosciutto and fry for 2–3 minutes, until crisp. Remove the prosciutto from the pan, leaving the oil in the pan, cool for a couple of minutes, then chop into bite-sized pieces. Pour any oil from the pan over the quinoa mixture.

4. Add the prosciutto and basil to the quinoa and toss gently to combine. Scatter the watercress and cheese over the top but do not mix. If transporting, cover the bowl.

5. Toss the watercress and cheese through the salad just before serving.

Shrimp cocktail in a jar

Serves 4

Serving food in jars has become very popular, but it's also a practical way of transporting a salad. You'll need four large, clean jars with lids. If you don't have any jars, you can simply serve the salad on a platter with the cocktail sauce spooned over. I much prefer to buy raw shrimp and cook them myself, but you can use cooked shrimp here. Buy the best quality egg mayonnaise you can find.

20 large raw shrimp (prawns), peeled and deveined, or 20 cooked peeled and deveined shrimp

150 g (5½ oz) mixed salad leaves

paprika, for dusting

lemon wedges, to serve

Shrimp cocktail sauce

40 g (1½ oz/¼ cup) good-quality egg mayonnaise

2 tablespoons sour cream

2 heaped teaspoons tomato sauce (ketchup)

dash of worcestershire sauce

couple of good shakes of Tabasco sauce

2 tablespoons lemon juice

1. If using raw shrimp, cook them in boiling water for about 3 minutes, or until they turn pink, then refresh under cold water. Cut each shrimp into bite-sized pieces.

2. Combine all the cocktail sauce ingredients. Add extra lemon juice, Tabasco and worcestershire sauce to taste, to make a full-flavoured, tangy sauce.

3. Divide half the salad leaves among the jars, then add half the shrimp. Top with the remaining salad leaves and remaining shrimp. Put a spoonful or two of cocktail sauce on top of the shrimp and sprinkle with paprika. Pop the lids on and seal tightly.

4. If not transporting immediately, place the jars in the fridge until needed. Mix the dressing into the salad before starting to eat. Offer the lemon wedges for squeezing over the salad.

TIP
To keep the jars safe while on the move, wrap each one in a large cloth napkin and secure with twine or a rubber band, tucking a fork into the side of each, then present each person with a still-wrapped jar.

Little Thai beef and noodle salads to go

Serves 6

This salad looks great served in bamboo or cardboard takeaway noodle boxes. Fill the boxes before you leave home, then hand them out at mealtime. For a bit of fun, offer chopsticks or search out some bamboo cutlery.

3 makrut (kaffir) lime leaves

5 cm (2 in) piece of lemongrass

1 garlic clove

5 cm (2 in) piece of ginger

2 teaspoons vegetable oil

1 teaspoon fish sauce

700–800 g (1 lb 9 oz–1 lb 12 oz) beef scotch fillet

1 tablespoon olive oil

375 g (13 oz) rice stick noodles

250 g (9 oz) cherry tomatoes, quartered

1 small red onion, cut in half and thinly sliced

large handful coriander (cilantro), leaves picked

large handful Thai basil or mint, leaves picked

Chilli-lime dressing

3 makrut (kaffir) lime leaves, thinly shredded

80 ml (2½ fl oz/⅓ cup) lime juice

2½ tablespoons fish sauce

3 teaspoons vegetable oil

1½ teaspoons sugar

1 small red chilli, deseeded and finely chopped

1. Roughly chop the lime leaves, lemongrass, garlic and ginger, and place in a spice grinder or small food processor with the oil and fish sauce. Grind to a paste. Rub the paste all over the beef and marinate in the fridge for at least 1 hour, or up to 4 hours.

2. Heat a chargrill pan over medium–high heat. Brush the beef with the olive oil and cook for 3–4 minutes on each side for medium–rare, or until cooked to your liking, bearing in mind that it will continue to cook while it rests. Cover with foil and set aside to rest for 10 minutes, then slice it very thinly against the grain.

3. Meanwhile, cook the noodles according to the packet instructions. Rinse under cold water, drain well and set aside.

4. Combine all the dressing ingredients in a small bowl. Pour about three-quarters of the dressing over the noodles and toss well, then leave to cool completely.

5. Divide the noodles among six noodle boxes (you may need to loosen the noodles a little using a couple of forks or tongs), then top with the cherry tomatoes, onion, herbs and beef. Alternatively, put the noodles in a leakproof container and top with the remaining ingredients. Take the remaining dressing in a separate container.

6. Serve the salad with a little extra dressing spooned over the top, mixing the salad gently as you eat.

Crushed potatoes with feta, pancetta, rocket and olives

Serves 4

This salad can be enjoyed as a meal on its own, or served as part of a selection of dishes.

800 g (1 lb 12 oz) small salad (new) potatoes, larger ones cut in half

2½ tablespoons olive oil

100 g (3½ oz) pancetta or prosciutto

2½ tablespoons lemon juice

handful flat-leaf (Italian) parsley, roughly chopped

small handful mint, roughly torn

20 pitted kalamata olives, cut in half

100 g (3½ oz) rocket (arugula)

180 g (6½ oz) Persian feta or other soft feta cheese, drained if in oil, and broken into small pieces

MAKE IT VEG

Simply omit the pancetta.

1. Put the potatoes in a large saucepan of salted water. Bring to the boil, then reduce the heat and simmer for about 15 minutes, or until the potatoes are tender when pierced with the tip of a sharp knife. Be careful not to overcook them.

2. Meanwhile, heat 1 teaspoon of the oil in a frying pan over medium heat. Add the pancetta and fry for 3–4 minutes, or until crisp. Remove from the pan and set aside.

3. Drain the potatoes well and leave to cool for 5–10 minutes. Transfer them to a clean tea towel (dish towel) and wrap them up. Using your palms, gently squash the potatoes to crack them open a little. Tip them into a large bowl.

4. While the potatoes are still warm, combine the lemon juice and remaining olive oil and season well with sea salt and freshly ground black pepper. Pour the mixture over the potatoes and toss gently to combine. Set aside to cool.

5. Roughly chop the fried pancetta, then add it to the cooled potatoes along with the parsley, mint, olives and rocket, tossing gently to combine. Scatter with the feta and serve.

6. If transporting, take the rocket and feta separately and toss through just before serving.

Fish fillets with crunchy Asian slaw

Serves 4–6

Most kids like sweet chilli sauce, so don't worry about the coleslaw being too spicy. This recipe is really all about the salad. If making this in advance, don't add the dressing until you are ready to serve, otherwise the cabbage will wilt.

4–6 fish fillets (about 180 g/6½ oz each), such as snapper or salmon

olive oil, for brushing

Asian slaw

juice of 1 lime

2 tablespoons fish sauce

2 tablespoons sweet chilli sauce

¼ Chinese cabbage or white cabbage, cored and finely shredded

¼ red cabbage, cored and finely shredded

1 carrot, grated

about 30 snow peas, trimmed and strings removed from one side, thinly sliced lengthways

1. To make the slaw, combine the lime juice, fish sauce and sweet chilli sauce in a large bowl. Add the cabbage, carrot and snow peas, and toss to combine. Set aside while cooking the fish.

2. Brush the fish all over with olive oil and season with salt and freshly ground black pepper. Cook the fish on a grill rack over a fire, or on a barbecue or in a chargrill pan or frying pan over medium–high heat for about 4 minutes on each side, or until just cooked through – the exact cooking time will depend on the thickness of the fish.

3. To serve, divide the coleslaw among serving plates and place a fillet of fish on top.

Kid-friendly

cooking

Simple chicken satay skewers

In my experience chicken is loved by pretty much every kid on the planet. Thrown together with their other all-time favourite, peanut butter, and you've got a winning combination. This is a great recipe to involve the kids in the cooking, just make sure they wash their hands before and after handling raw chicken.

8–10 metal or wooden skewers

400 ml (14 oz) tin coconut milk

1 tablespoon soy sauce

700 g (1 lb 9 oz) skinless, boneless chicken breast, preferably free-range, cut into cubes or 6 cm (2½ in) strips

100 g (3½ oz/⅓ cup) crunchy or smooth peanut butter

1. If using wooden skewers, soak them in cold water for about 20 minutes beforehand to prevent them burning. Combine about half of the coconut milk with the soy sauce in a large bowl. Add the chicken, toss to coat and leave to marinate for about 20 minutes in the fridge or a cool box.

2. Thread the chicken onto skewers, discarding the leftover marinade. Place the skewers on a barbeque over medium heat or on an oiled grill rack over a part of a fire that isn't too hot, so the chicken doesn't burn on the outside before it cooks on the inside.

3. Cook the chicken for about 10 minutes, or until just cooked through. Do not overcook or it will become dry.

4. When the chicken is almost cooked, heat the remaining coconut milk and the peanut butter in a small saucepan, stirring regularly, until it is bubbling and thickened. Serve the skewers with the warm satay sauce on the side. Or cook over medium heat on a barbecue.

TIP
You can also make four
large burgers. Cook
them for 5–6 minutes
on each side.

Cheesy beef burgers

Make sure everyone's hands are clean before they start mixing together these really simple burgers. Once the patties have cooked, the kids will enjoy designing their own burger, using slices of cheese, tomato, gherkins and salad – or not!

Beef patties

1 small onion, finely chopped

1 garlic clove, crushed

600 g (1 lb 5 oz) minced beef

100 g (3½ oz/1 cup) finely grated cheddar, tasty or parmesan cheese

2 tablespoons olive oil

To serve

8 small burger buns or 16 slices of bread

tomato sauce (ketchup)

good-quality egg mayonnaise

slices of cheese

slices of tomato

slices of gherkin or cucumber

salad leaves

1. Put the onion, garlic, beef and cheese into a large bowl and season with salt and freshly ground black pepper. Use your hands to mix everything together well, squishing and mixing the mince until it turns a slightly pink colour. Divide the meat into eight even-sized portions and shape each portion into a patty.

2. Heat the oil in a frying pan over medium–high heat or on a grill rack over a fire, on a gas cooker or on a barbecue flatplate. Arrange the burgers in a single layer and cook for 3–4 minutes on each side, or until the burgers are cooked through. The cooking time will depend on the thickness of the burgers and the heat of your fire.

3. Briefly toast the buns or bread to warm through, then add a beef patty and your choice of sauces and toppings.

Beef or chicken kebabs

You can make these kebabs using either chicken or beef. Although chicken thigh meat takes longer to cook than breast meat when grilled, it stays moister. If using beef, select a tender cut, such as fillet. There are lots of filling suggestions; let the kids put them out on a serving platter and choose what they like.

8 metal or wooden skewers

2 tablespoons olive oil

2 tablespoons honey

2 tablespoons wholegrain mustard

700–800 g (1 lb 9 oz–1 lb 12 oz) beef fillets or skinless, boneless chicken thigh or breast fillets, preferably free-range, cut into 2 cm (¾ in) cubes

8 pita breads

To serve

Lebanese (short) cucumbers, cut into batons

grated carrot

grated cheese

cherry tomatoes, quartered

sliced avocado

lettuce leaves

1. If using wooden skewers, soak them in water for 20 minutes before using to prevent them burning during cooking. Combine the olive oil, honey and mustard in a large bowl to make a marinade. Add the chicken or beef pieces to the bowl and mix well to coat. If you have time, set aside in the fridge or a cool box for 1 hour to let the flavours develop.

2. Thread the meat onto the skewers, so each cube of meat is just touching, but not too tightly packed.

3. Cook the kebabs on a grill rack over a fire or directly on a barbecue for 12–15 minutes, turning regularly. Ensure the chicken is cooked through before serving, although beef can be served a little rare.

4. Sit the pita breads briefly over the fire or barbecue to warm through and soften. Carefully pull the meat off the skewers and split open each pita bread. Add your choice of fillings, and serve.

MAKE IT VEG

Alternate cubes of haloumi and cherry tomatoes on the skewers, brush with oil and grill.

Crumbed chicken with sticky dipping sauce

Makes about 15

The large, crisp panko breadcrumbs used in this recipe give the chicken a really crisp coating, while the dipping sauce is rich, sticky and totally delicious!

1–2 free-range eggs

90 g (3 oz/1½ cups) panko (Japanese breadcrumbs) (*see* Tip page 3)

2 tablespoons finely chopped coriander (cilantro)

800 g (1 lb 12 oz) boneless, skinless chicken breasts, preferably free-range, cut into long strips or bite-sized pieces

vegetable oil, for shallow frying

Sticky dipping sauce

1 tablespoon vegetable oil

2 garlic cloves, crushed

2 teaspoons finely grated ginger

60 ml (2 fl oz/¼ cup) hoisin sauce

60 ml (2 fl oz/¼ cup) sweet chilli sauce

1. Make the dipping sauce first to allow it time to cool. Heat the oil in a small frying pan, then add the garlic and ginger and fry gently for about 2 minutes. Add the remaining ingredients, 2 tablespoons water and a good grinding of freshly ground black pepper (no salt). Stir to combine, then bring to the boil. Remove from the heat and leave to cool. This sauce will keep for 2–3 days in an airtight container in the fridge.

2. Lightly beat one of the eggs in a shallow dish. Combine the panko and coriander in a bowl, season with sea salt and freshly ground black pepper, then tip half onto a large plate.

3. Preheat the oven to 160°C (320°F) fan-forced. Dip each piece of chicken into the beaten egg, allowing any excess to drip off, then dip into the panko mixture, coating on all sides. Use the second egg and remaining panko as needed — keeping it in two batches stops the breadcrumbs becoming soggy!

4. Heat 1–2 cm (1 in) vegetable oil in a large frying pan over medium–high heat. Cook the chicken in batches, being careful not to overcrowd the pan, for 2–3 minutes on each side, until golden brown and cooked through. Drain on paper towel, then keep warm in the oven while cooking the remaining chicken.

5. Serve warm or cold, with the dipping sauce.

6. If taking these somewhere that has a stove, you may like to take them raw but ready crumbed, then cook on arrival. Or you could cook them at home, then reheat them in the oven before serving.

Chocolate chip cookies

These are my absolute favourite cookies. They should be soft and chewy, not hard and crumbly. I often make a large batch and freeze half, ready shaped and uncooked, so I always have some in the freezer ready to bake. Stored in an airtight container they should last up to five days, but they are irresistibly more-ish and for this reason come with a warning!

275 g (9½ oz/1¾ cups) plain (all-purpose) flour

1 teaspoon salt

1 teaspoon baking powder

225 g (8 oz) butter, softened

175 g (6 oz/¾ cup firmly packed) brown sugar

175 g (6 oz/¾ cup) caster (superfine) sugar

2 free-range eggs, lightly beaten

200 g (7 oz/1¼ cups) chocolate chips

100 g (3½ oz/¾ cup) mixed nuts, chopped

1 teaspoon natural vanilla extract

1. Sift the flour, salt and baking powder into a large bowl.

2. In a separate bowl, beat together the butter and both sugars with an electric hand mixer for 4–5 minutes, or until pale and creamy. Gradually beat in the eggs, mixing well after each addition. Don't worry if the mixture starts to curdle.

3. Slowly add the flour mixture and stir until well combined. Stir in the chocolate chips, nuts and vanilla extract. Leave to chill in the fridge for 1–2 hours. Although they can be baked immediately, chilling them gives the cookies a better shape and texture.

4. Preheat the oven to 180°C (350°F) fan-forced. Line two baking trays with baking paper. Take heaped teaspoon-sized portions of the cookie mixture and quickly roll them into balls, then flatten slightly. Place on the trays about 5 cm (2 in) apart. Bake for 10–15 minutes, or until golden, but soft.

5. Remove from the oven and leave the cookies to cool on the trays for 5 minutes before transferring to a wire rack to cool completely. Store in an airtight container for up to 5 days.

TIP
It's fine to make these nut-free, just add an extra 100 g (3½ oz) of chocolate chips.

TIP

You can bake these in a smaller 16 × 16 cm (6 × 6 in) tin, but allow 30–35 minutes to cook, as the brownies will be thicker. If using a larger tin than suggested, bake the brownies for 15–20 minutes, but bear in mind they won't be quite as moist.

Chocolate brownies

(V)

These brownies are chewy and delicious – you can choose whether to make them even more decadent by adding chocolate chips, or more 'adult' by adding nuts – I often add hazelnuts, but unsalted macadamias are great too. Sometimes I cut these brownies into tiny squares to make them a one-bite treat. It's easiest to cut them into 16 squares first and then halve each one.

185 ml (6 fl oz/¾ cup) vegetable oil

230 g (8 oz/1½ cups lightly packed) brown sugar

2 free-range eggs, lightly beaten

1 teaspoon natural vanilla extract

100 g (3½ oz/⅔ cup) chocolate chips (or chopped walnuts, hazelnuts or unsalted macadamia nuts)

75 g (2½ oz/½ cup) plain (all-purpose) flour

¼ teaspoon baking powder

40 g (1½ oz/⅓ cup) unsweetened cocoa powder

1. Preheat the oven to 180°C (350°F) fan-forced. Grease and line the base and sides of a 21 × 21 cm (8 × 8 in) cake tin (*see* Tip).

2. Put the oil and sugar in a large bowl and whisk using an electric hand mixer for about 2 minutes until well combined. Add the eggs and vanilla extract and whisk until just blended. Stir in the chocolate chips or nuts and distribute evenly.

3. Sift the flour, baking powder and cocoa into the mixture and fold in, but do not over-mix. Pour into the prepared tin and bake for about 20 minutes. To test if the brownies are cooked, insert a skewer into the middle – it should come out a bit gooey but not have any raw mixture on it.

4. Remove from the oven and allow to cool in the tin for 5 minutes, then carefully lift out using the baking paper and transfer to a wire rack to cool completely. Trim the edges (eating them of course), then cut into 16 or 20 pieces. The brownies can be stored in an airtight container for up to four days, but will start to lose their moistness the longer they are kept.

A bit of fun with cupcakes

This is great for a party, at the campsite or on a picnic. Bake some cupcakes and make the frosting beforehand, then let the kids decorate their cupcakes with sprinkles, chocolate flakes or your preferred toppings. Any leftover frosting is delicious on toast or in sandwiches!

Cupcakes

100 g (3½ oz) butter, softened

185 g (6½ oz) caster (superfine) sugar

½ teaspoon natural vanilla extract

2 free-range eggs

125 ml (4 fl oz/½ cup) milk

200 g (7 oz/1⅓ cups) self-raising flour

Frosting

250 g (9 oz) cream cheese

3 tablespoons strawberry jam

Decorations

sprinkles

chocolate flake, crumbled

mini M&Ms

other edible decorations

1. Preheat the oven to 180°C (350°F) fan-forced and line a standard 12-hole (80 ml/2½ fl oz/⅓ cup capacity) muffin tin with paper cases.

2. Put the butter, sugar and vanilla extract into a bowl and beat with an electric hand mixer, until pale and soft.

3. Add the eggs, one at a time, and beat until just combined. Add the milk and flour alternately in small amounts and stir with a wooden spoon until just combined. Do not over-mix.

4. Divide the mixture evenly among the paper cases, then bake for 15–20 minutes, or until cooked and golden on top. Remove from the oven, leave in the tin for 5 minutes, then transfer to a wire rack to cool completely. Store in an airtight container.

5. To make the frosting, soften the cream cheese with a spoon or a fork, then add the jam and mix to combine. Put the different sprinkles and chocolate into separate small bowls. Put the cupcakes out and let the kids decorate them, spreading first with the cream cheese frosting, using a blunt knife, and then adding their favourite toppings. Don't worry about how good they look, let the kids go crazy with the sprinkles.

Something

sweet

Pistachio meringues with caramel filling

I love meringues; they're a favourite from Sunday afternoon tea when I was a child. Instead of the traditional cream filling, I've filled these ones with caramel. Look for caramel in a tin in the baking section of supermarkets, or you can easily make your own caramel using condensed milk.

4 free-range egg whites

220 g (8 oz) caster (superfine) sugar

2 teaspoons cornflour (cornstarch)

1 teaspoon white vinegar

40 g (1½ oz/⅓ cup) roughly chopped pistachio nuts

Caramel filling

380 g (13½ oz) caramel in a tin, or a 395 g (14 oz) tin of condensed milk

1. If you don't have tinned caramel, make the caramel filling first. Remove the label from the condensed milk tin and make two small holes in the top. Place the tin upright in a saucepan. Pour enough water into the saucepan to sit 2 cm (¾ in) below the top of the tin, being careful not to let any water into the holes. Bring to a simmer, uncovered, and keep simmering for 4 hours. You'll need to keep an eye on the water level and top it up with boiling water as necessary. Never let the pan run dry, otherwise your tin may explode! Carefully remove the tin from the pan and leave to cool completely.

2. Meanwhile, preheat the oven to 140°C (275°F) fan-forced, and line three baking sheets with baking paper. Put the egg whites in a clean, grease-free bowl and, using a stand mixer or electric hand mixer, beat them until soft peaks form. Gradually add the sugar, 1 tablespoon at a time, whisking well after each addition. Whisk until the mixture is smooth and glossy. Fold in the cornflour, vinegar and three-quarters of the pistachios.

3. Put the mixture into a piping (icing) bag with no tube, or into a zip-lock bag with the corner snipped off. Pipe small mounds, about 5 cm (2 in) in diameter, onto the baking sheets, allowing a little room in between each for expansion, and sprinkle with the remaining pistachios.

4. Reduce the oven temperature to 130°C (265°F) fan-forced and bake for 40 minutes. Turn the oven off and leave the meringues inside to cool completely.

5. Scoop the caramel out of the tin, whisking it briefly to soften. Use it to carefully sandwich the meringues together.

6. These meringues are fine to transport filled. Don't squash them into a tin, but equally ensure they don't have too much room to move about, otherwise they may break.

Raspberry cake

If you're not a particularly confident baker, this is the cake for you — it looks great but is pretty simple to make. Fresh or frozen raspberries can be used, so it can be made all year round (I actually prefer to use frozen as they're often juicier). Serve it as a simple slice of cake or with a dollop of cream as more of a dessert.

120 g (4½ oz) salted butter, softened, plus extra for greasing

225 g (8 oz/1½ cups) plain (all-purpose) flour, plus extra for dusting

185 g (6½ oz/1 cup lightly packed) brown sugar

3 free-range eggs, lightly beaten

60 ml (2 fl oz/¼ cup) milk

grated zest of 1 orange

2 tablespoons orange juice

1 teaspoon baking powder

200 g (7 oz) fresh raspberries, or thawed frozen raspberries

icing (confectioners') sugar, for dusting

thickened (double) cream, to serve (optional)

1. Preheat the oven to 180°C (350°F) fan-forced. Butter and lightly flour the side of a 23 cm (9 in) springform or loose-based cake tin.

2. Using a stand mixer or electric hand mixer, beat the butter and sugar for 4–5 minutes, until creamy. Gradually add the eggs, beating well after each addition, then whisk in the milk. The mixture may look like it has curdled, but it should be fine when the flour is added.

3. Stir in the orange zest and juice, then sift in the flour and baking powder and fold through. Gently fold half the raspberries through. Spoon the mixture into the cake tin, smoothing the top. Scatter the remaining raspberries over the top, pressing them gently into the batter.

4. Bake for 30 minutes, or until the cake has risen and is golden and a skewer comes out clean. Leave in the tin to cool for 10 minutes, then remove from the tin and cool on a wire rack. Dust with icing sugar and serve in slices, accompanied by cream, if desired. This cake is best eaten the day it is made.

5. If transporting, return the cake to the tin to keep it safe.

Bread and butter pudding in the fire

This is the perfect way to use up any leftover bread, as bits and pieces from different loaves can be used. If cream isn't available, use all milk instead. If a sweeter pudding is preferred, spread the bread with some jam when buttering. On a camping trip one Easter we used sliced, leftover hot cross buns and it was absolutely divine.

softened butter, for greasing and spreading

8 slices of bread, halved

jam, for spreading (optional)

60 g (2 oz/⅓ cup) sultanas (optional)

3 eggs

3 tablespoons sugar

300 ml (10 fl oz/1¼ cups) thickened (double) or whipping cream (or an additional 300 ml (10 fl oz/ 1¼ cups) milk)

375 ml (12½ fl oz/ 1½ cups) milk

1. Lightly grease a large camp oven (or fire-proof dish with a lid) with butter.

2. Spread each slice of bread with butter and jam, if using, and arrange in the dish in layers from front to back so the slices are standing up against each other. Scatter over the sultanas, if using.

3. Using a whisk or fork, whisk together the eggs, sugar, cream and milk until well combined. Slowly pour over the bread, letting the bread soak up the liquid a little. Set aside for 10 minutes to allow a little more soaking.

4. Put the lid on the camp oven or dish, then sit on the edge of the fire surrounded by coals. Make sure there are no coals underneath the oven or it will burn the base of the pudding. Leave for about 30 minutes, or until the custard has set. Alternatively, you can cook this pudding in a covered barbecue with only the outside burners turned on low.

5. Remove from the heat and serve immediately.

MAKE AT HOME

Follow the instructions above, but bake in a baking dish (about 5 cm/2 in deep) in a preheated oven (180°C/350°F fan-forced) for 30–35 minutes.

Strawberry and passionfruit meringue cake

Serves 8

Meringue always looks impressive, and this slightly chewy version filled with strawberries and a hint of passionfruit is no exception.

6 free-range egg whites, at room temperature

250 g (9 oz) caster (superfine) sugar

1½ teaspoons white vinegar

1 teaspoon natural vanilla extract

35 g (1¼ oz/⅓ cup) ground hazelnuts

icing (confectioners') sugar, for dusting

Filling

300 ml (10 fl oz/1¼ cups) thickened (double) or pouring (whipping) cream

2 passionfruit, cut in half

250 g (9 oz) strawberries, hulled and roughly chopped

1. Preheat the oven to 140°C (275°F) fan-forced. Line two baking sheets with baking paper, then draw a 22 cm (8¾ in) circle on each. Turn the paper over, so the drawings are face down.

2. Using a stand mixer or electric hand mixer, whisk the egg whites in a clean, grease-free bowl until stiff peaks form. Gradually add the sugar, whisking well after each addition to dissolve the sugar. Continue beating until the mixture is thick and glossy. Briefly whisk in the vinegar and vanilla extract. Gently fold in the ground hazelnuts.

3. Spoon the mixture onto the two baking paper circles, smoothing the surface. Bake for 35–40 minutes, then turn the oven off and leave the meringues to cool completely in the oven.

4. To make the filling, whisk the cream until stiff peaks form, then scoop out the passionfruit pulp and stir into the cream.

5. Remove the baking paper and place one meringue disc on a serving plate. Spread the cream and passionfruit mixture over the disc and scatter the strawberries over the top. Top with the second meringue disc and dust with icing sugar.

6. If you don't feel confident transporting the cake assembled, take the meringues and filling separately and put everything together on arrival – wrap the meringues in foil and carefully place them in a box padded out with tea towels. Remember to bring the icing sugar for dusting.

Nectarine puff pastry tartlets with frangipane filling

Makes 8

(V)

Nectarines are one of my favourite summer fruits; I love them especially for their amazing colours. I also love the purple tinge of the pistachios used in this recipe, but it's fine if you don't want to add them.

2 sheets frozen puff pastry, about 24 × 24 cm (9½ × 9½ in), thawed in fridge

4 firm, ripe nectarines, stoned and cut into eight wedges

2 tablespoons apricot jam, melted

35 g (1¼ oz/¼ cup) roughly chopped pistachio nuts (optional)

1 small free-range egg, lightly beaten

icing (confectioners') sugar, for dusting (optional)

Frangipane filling

50 g (1¾ oz) unsalted butter

50 g (1¾ oz/¼ cup) caster (superfine) sugar

1 small free-range egg, lightly beaten

50 g (1¾ oz/½ cup) ground almonds

1 tablespoon plain (all-purpose) flour

½ teaspoon natural almond extract

1. To make the frangipane filling, put the butter and sugar in a food processor and blend for about 30 seconds, until creamed together. Add the egg, ground almonds, flour and almond extract and blend well, scraping down the sides of the bowl once. Transfer to a small bowl.

2. Preheat the oven to 180°C (350°F) fan-forced. Line two baking trays with baking paper. Cut each puff pastry sheet into quarters. Using a sharp knife, cut a shallow border 1 cm (⅓ in) from the edge of each piece, ensuring you don't cut all the way through the pastry; this will enable the pastry border to puff up around the filling when it bakes. Place on the baking trays. Spread the frangipane filling inside the border, then chill for 15 minutes.

3. Top the frangipane with the nectarine slices, brush with the jam and scatter with pistachios, if using. Brush the pastry borders with the beaten egg. Bake for 20 minutes, or until the tartlets are puffed and golden.

4. Serve warm or cold, dusted with icing sugar, if you like.

5. If transporting, either bake the tartlets beforehand and serve them cold on arrival, or, if you're going somewhere with an oven, assemble and chill them before leaving home, then bake them at your destination.

Lemon and passionfruit melting moments

Here's one for kids and adults alike. If you don't like passionfruit seeds, sieve them before adding the passionfruit pulp to the butter and lemon zest.

250 g (9 oz) butter, at room temperature

50 g (1¾ oz) icing (confectioners') sugar, sifted

1 teaspoon natural vanilla extract

250 g (9 oz/1⅔ cups) plain (all-purpose) flour, plus a little extra for dusting

60 g (2 oz/1½ cup) cornflour (cornstarch)

Filling

2 passionfruit, cut in half

60 g (2 oz) butter, at room temperature

finely grated zest of 1 lemon

110 g (4 oz) icing (confectioners') sugar, sifted

1. Preheat the oven to 150°C (300°F) fan-forced, and line two baking sheets with baking paper. Using a stand mixer or electric hand mixer, whisk the butter, icing sugar and vanilla extract together for 4–5 minutes, until pale and creamy. Sift the plain flour and cornflour and, with the mixer on a very low speed, gradually whisk into the butter mixture. Stop mixing when it is just combined and you have a soft dough.

2. Lightly flour your hands, then take teaspoon-sized portions of the mixture and roll them into balls. Place on the baking sheets, about 5 cm (2 in) apart. Dip a fork into some flour, then gently flatten each ball to about 1 cm (½ in) thick. Bake for 18–20 minutes, or until the biscuits are very light golden. Leave to cool on the baking sheets.

3. Meanwhile, make the filling. Scoop the passionfruit pulp into a bowl with the butter and lemon zest. Using an electric hand mixer, whisk until combined. Add half the icing sugar and whisk again until combined, then whisk in the remaining icing sugar until the sugar has dissolved. Refrigerate until it has firmed up, about 30 minutes to 1 hour.

4. Spread half the biscuits with a layer of the filling, then sandwich together with a second biscuit. Store in an airtight container until required; they should last 3–4 days.

Orange and almond choc-truffle squares

These are extremely rich and absolutely divine, so you only need a small piece: a little goes a long way.

vegetable oil, for greasing

100 g (3½ oz) slivered almonds

150 ml (5 fl oz) pouring (single/light) cream

200 g (7 oz) good-quality 70% dark chocolate, broken into pieces

200 g (7 oz) good-quality 70% orange dark chocolate, broken into pieces

50 g (1¾ oz) butter, diced

Dutch (unsweetened) cocoa powder, for dusting

1. Grease a 16 × 16 cm (6¼ × 6¼ in) tin (or one with similar dimensions) and line with baking paper.

2. Toast the almonds in a dry frying pan over medium heat for 2–3 minutes, until lightly golden. Set aside to cool.

3. Pour the cream into a small saucepan and bring just to the boil. While the cream is heating, put both the chocolates in a heatproof bowl over a saucepan of barely simmering water, ensuring the bowl doesn't touch the water.

4. Pour the cream over the chocolate. Add the butter and stir gently every now and then to melt the chocolate and combine well. Do not overheat the chocolate, or it will seize and be ruined. When the chocolate is completely melted, remove from the heat and stir until lovely and glossy, then stir in the toasted almonds.

5. Pour into the prepared tin, then refrigerate for 2–3 hours, or until firm.

6. Carefully remove the truffle from the tin and dust with cocoa powder. Using a sharp knife, cut into 4 × 2 cm (1¼ × ¾ in) pieces, cleaning the knife every so often. If taking it on a picnic, you might find it easiest to return it to the tin to transport. Keep it out of the sun!

TIP
Wrap a few squares of this truffle in baking paper and tie with twine. It's the perfect way to say thank you, happy birthday or merry Christmas.

Hazelnut and raspberry roulade

Many roulades are made from meringue, but that type can be quite hard to roll. This one is softer and more cake-like, so is easier to roll and transport. It may crack slightly but that's fine — just dust the crack with extra icing sugar! You can also fill it with chopped strawberries or blackberries.

vegetable oil, for greasing

6 free-range eggs, separated

180 g (6½ oz/¾ cup) caster (superfine) sugar, plus extra for sprinkling

1 teaspoon natural vanilla extract

50 g (1¾ oz/⅓ cup) self-raising flour

75 g (2½ oz/⅔ cup) ground hazelnuts

icing (confectioners') sugar, for dusting

Filling

1 tablespoon icing (confectioners') sugar

150 ml (5½ oz) thickened (double) or pouring (whipping)

100 g (3½ oz) crème fraîche or sour cream

½ teaspoon natural vanilla extract

125 g (4½ oz) fresh raspberries, or thawed frozen raspberries

1. Preheat the oven to 180°C (350°F) fan-forced. Grease a Swiss roll (jelly roll) tin, about 30 × 24 × 2½ cm (12 × 9½ × 1 in). Line with baking paper.

2. Put the egg yolks and sugar in a large bowl. Using a stand mixer or electric hand mixer, whisk for 5–6 minutes, until pale and thick. Stir in the vanilla extract. Sift in the flour, then fold in gently with the ground hazelnuts.

3. Using clean beaters, whisk the egg whites in a separate bowl until soft peaks form. Gently fold into the hazelnut mixture with a large metal spoon until just combined. Pour into the prepared tin. Bake for 15–20 minutes until golden and springy.

4. Place a tea towel (dish towel) on a work surface, top it with a large sheet of baking paper and sprinkle with caster sugar. Carefully turn the roulade out onto the sugared paper, then carefully peel off the paper that was in the baking tin. Trim the edges of the roulade to neaten, if necessary. Using the sugared paper to help you, roll up the roulade from the long side, enclosing the paper as you go. Leave to cool completely.

5. To make the filling, sift the icing sugar into the cream, then whisk until soft peaks form. Fold in the crème fraîche and vanilla extract. Gently stir the raspberries through.

6. Unroll the roulade and spread with the raspberry cream filling. Re-roll the roulade. Place on a serving plate and dust with icing sugar. If transporting, dust with icing sugar just before serving.

Index

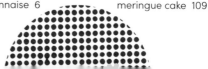

Acknowledgements

Putting a cookbook together is always great fun and this one was no exception. As usual it was a team effort, so much thanks must go to the team. Firstly, a massive thank you to my editor Helena Holmgren who really helped pull this book into shape. As another avid camper and eater of food outdoors, it was great to collaborate with you. Thank you for all your great suggestions for the book, they were very much appreciated.

Thanks to the team at Hardie Grant – my project editor Megan Cuthbert who kept the process calm and simple and my publisher Melissa Kayser. Melissa, you've been with me on my book publishing journey now for almost 10 years, thank you for your continued support of me and my books.

Thank you George Saad for your great book design and for all your help with the cover. Thank you to Peter, Miranda, Priscilla and George for your modelling skills.

And a final thank you to my kids Max and Jack and to all my great friends who continue to inspire me to cook outside. Cooking and eating outdoors with you all is my happy place.

About the author

With a long and successful career as a food writer and stylist, Katy Holder has always been passionate about cooking and encouraging people to cook. Katy grew up in London but has lived in Sydney for many years, where the weather allows her to indulge her love of eating outdoors with her two teenage boys and her friends. She is the author of 10 cookbooks (including *The Hungry Campers Cookbook* and *A Moveable Feast*). She has been the Food Director of *Family Circle Magazine*, wrote the food pages for Australian *marie claire* magazine for several years and has written for most leading Australian and UK food magazines. Katy also works for Marley Spoon, one of Australia's leading meal-kit delivery companies.

Some of the material in this book originally appeared in Hungry Campers Cookbook and A Moveable Feast, published by Hardie Grant Travel, 2017, and where full acknowledgements for individual contributions appear.

Image page VII Unsplash; page XV Katy Holder

Published in 2021 by Hardie Grant Explore,
a division of Hardie Grant Publishing

Hardie Grant Explore (Melbourne)
Wurundjeri Country
Building 1, 658 Church Street
Richmond, Victoria 3121

Hardie Grant Explore (Sydney)
Gadigal Country
Level 7, 45 Jones Street
Ultimo, NSW 2007

www.hardiegrant.com/au/travel

A catalogue record for this book is available from the National Library of Australia

NATIONAL LIBRARY OF AUSTRALIA

Hardie Grant acknowledges the Traditional Owners of the Country on which we work, the Wurundjeri people of the Kulin Nation and the Gadigal people of the Eora Nation, and recognises their continuing connection to the land, waters and culture. We pay our respects to their Elders past, present and emerging.

Good Food Outdoors
ISBN 9781741177688

10 9 8 7 6 5 4 3 2 1

Publisher Melissa Kayser
Project editor Megan Cuthbert
Editor Helena Holmgren
Proofreader Rosanna Dutson
Design George Saad
Cover photography Chris Chen
Typesetting Hannah Schubert
Index Max McMaster

Printed in China by 1010 Printing International Limited